REFLECTIONS ON THE WATER

FORTY DAYS OF PRAYING AND PONDERING THROUGH LENT

BARBARA GLASSON

KEVIN MAYHEW LTD

First published in 2020 by Kevin Mayhew Ltd,
Rattlesden,
Stowmarket,
Suffolk, IP14 3BW
www.kevinmayhew.com

ISBN: 978-1-8385-8088-9 (Paperback edition)
ISBN: 978-1-8385-8089-6 (eBook edition)

Created with Vellum

CONTENTS

but also to revisit some of my memories of family and childhood.

I have been contemplating the primal place of water in our physical environment and in our spiritual landscape. Like many I have always been drawn to the edge and to the sea, from a childhood close to the Kent coast, to ministry in Liverpool, from the children's paddling pool to the Rohingya refugee camps of Myanmar and Bangladesh. At the beginning of Lent we find Jesus in a wilderness, parched and alone, a thirsty human in a dry land. In these reflections and prayers I bring doubts and questions about what sustains life, faith and discipleship in dry places. And I also take a whimsical look at our world-wide relationship with water, the power it provides and the challenge for justice it presents.

I hope that what I have written will cause you to reflect along with me on this ordinary element that so shapes our lives and to find it quenches your thirst too!

INTRODUCTION

It is the beginning of Lent, a time to ponder and pray, to keep watch and to wait. This day stands on one foot, in the liminal space between winter and spring. As if we hadn't had enough of these short days and chaotic weather fronts, now is a time for the purple shrouding of the hopeful stories we had been anticipating. After months of hunkering down we are asked to dig deeper into our lives, to enter the desert for a further forty days and nights. To watch and wait in the garden, when surely we could just do with seeing the grass poke its pointed fingers towards the warming sun?

These forty reflections were written during the lockdown of the Covid 19 pandemic, when Lent and Easter took a different pace, when the unexpected confinement of the disease gave space and time to reflect more deeply than in the usual rush of days. They were written during my year as President of the Methodist Conference, a year of travel and challenge before being grounded. They have given me a chance to reflect not only my own experiences and travels

1

THE FIRST DAY - ASH WEDNESDAY.

Our dishwasher broke today. Well, not entirely, it simply announced by means of a tap symbol that it had entered 'flood mode'. Most people send for plumbers in such circumstances, for some reason this never occurs to us. We pulled it out from under the work surface and with a screwdriver in one hand and a Google help page in the other, we set about mending the fault. Now it's bedtime and it is on a test cycle whilst we slump exhausted into bed.

We never used to have a dishwasher. We used to take it in turns to 'wash or dry' it was part of the cycle of the week, negotiating the daily disputes of growing children. Then we saw a second hand one for sale for £50, now it seems indispensable. If this one doesn't make it through the night then we will soon be off to find a replacement. Strange how such a luxurious thing has become a seeming necessity, after all it is just a cupboard for dirty dishes.

This morning's liturgy marked us with the sign of the cross, a thumb print of contrition on the furrowed brows that tried to mend the dishwasher. This carbon thumbprint, inscribed as a mark of penitence in this disposable world. What stories we tell ourselves about what is indispensable!

In Zimbabwe I visited a project providing clean water to rural communities. The people of the village showed us the well, deep dug in the parched earth, plummeting to a underground source that would give life, health, possibility to the village.

We saw a hand washing system involving a plastic bottle, balanced between a string and operating from an improvised foot pedal, a 'tippy tap'. Simple alternative technology which we could see transformed this world to a place with great possibility. With clean water the broiler chickens gave the village women an income whilst the men sought work or other opportunities in the city. A simple ration of water, flowing from under the earth.

Dust to dust, ashes to ashes, we live in sure and certain hope that our life is a fragile gift, not to be squandered or taken for granted. And we are marked by this dry dust, that reminds us each day of our mortality. If only this forehead stigmata would be the source of living water for all God's people. If only, the carbon between my eyebrows would reconfigure my life into the simple equation of love for the whole Earth.

Today a carbon thumbprint
a smut on the face
of this tired and parched earth
ashes to ashes
blowing our shameful greed
dust to dust
calling us to repent.

Let our lenten footprints
be for trees and greening
for fresh and cleaner air
for sharing of this holy time
for lighter steps on this
precious earth
for life, for everyone.

Night One

Three o'clock in the morning, the earth turns its face to the wall and tries to sleep. The first hours have released the worries from the lid of exhaustion.

I wonder what it was like for Jesus on those cold desert nights, alone and thirsty under the vast expanse of the star-lit sky. Is that when the devil stalked him most, when all those 'if' questions prowled like wild beasts.?

I listen to the rain beat the breast of the window, lacrimose clouds blanketing my temperate homeland, the majestic dome of the sky obscured by the sulphurous glow of sentinel street lamps. Yet, I also live in a desert of doubt.

To counter my own resentful wakefulness I call others to mind, all those whose tears come at night, filling kettles in cold kitchens, those thirsty for meaning or forgiveness or forgetfulness.

I think of God's creation from 'The Deep', separating light from darkness, chaos from order, sea from land. God who holds back the oceans of grief and regret, who waters our dry souls with hope.

God of the ocean's deep
In these night hours

still the storms of our restless minds
raise us from the suction
of these eddies of self doubt
bring us by your presence
to the calm shores
of restful sleep.

2

THE SECOND DAY - THURSDAY

I am thinking about my Mum and how she died. It wasn't a tragedy, she was 90 and had seen her children and grandchildren into the world. She had a strong faith and a strong heart. She died very slowly from a bad case of old age. She simply became frailer and smaller and gave the impression of someone that was evaporating.

Mum loved the water. She had grown up in Chester and her favourite occupation was to take a rowing boat on the river Dee. In fact, that was a very important part of her courtship with Dad, I believe she rowed him upstream! She loved the alternative space she found when on water, the sense of being free and strong and bouyant. Of all the characters in the Wind in the Willows, she was the Water Rat. For Mum there was nothing more joyful than 'messing around in boats'.

So, I guess there was nothing strange about her evaporation. It wasn't so much that her body was turning to dust, as it was becoming water again. She wasn't leaving, she was returning. Returning somewhere where she could be connected again with all that happiness, that freedom, that bouyancy. Mum's dying was an ok thing. She had had enough. So much of who she was on whom she loved had already taken flight. Death is a bird on the wing, a seabird, rising to coast on a thermal, rising high over the ocean, soaring.

I miss her though. The suck of the waves through the Dungerness shingle will bring her to my heart's mind. That return to the fluid memories of innocence and longing. The waves of reminiscence of childhood and unanswered questions.

So Mum, like so many old ones returned to the edge. Looked out over the horizons and into another world. Pondering the ships that weigh anchor and set sail, eventually she relinquished life to join them. They call it 'Costa Geriatrica' but maybe that is to diminish the soul's call back to the amniotic fluid, the breaking of the waters into another dimension. The siren call of water. The return to the beginning to a primal memory of when the ocean was formed and life created us.

You took bread and fish
and broke and shared it
with those who imagined
they could walk on water.
You invited us,
over the Deep,
to this simple feast,
this breaking of waves and hearts,
this shoreline love,
this call to the other side.

Night Two

There is a ritual to the night. First, the agreement that this liturgy should commence. Then the walking and settling of the dog. The fire guard on sentry duty for the embers, the clearing of surfaces and the day's debris stacked. Then the closing down of things, of laptops, lights and all unfinished business. The closing of curtains. Checking the bins are out, the uniforms are ready, the alarm is set, the phone is on charge, and then, the turning of the head on the pillow ... and the closing of eyes.

First there is the opening of the taps
and the dangle of fingers into the mix
then the adding of salts,
the agitation that dissolves the crystals
meanwhile, the shedding of garments
some for washing, some for another day.
The final test, the hand, the foot,
the body sinks deep into the embrace
of the bath's forgiveness,
toes float away their callouses,
spine releases its responsibility,
shoulders find their fulcrum,
total immersion.
Could it be that,
in the simplicity of this daily baptism,
we discover what grace is like?

3

THE THIRD DAY - FRIDAY

I am not sure about giving a storm a name. A storm is not a person, not an equal, not a domestic animal - a storm is a wild thing, a rattler of cages. A storm is uncontrollable, it swirls and snaps. The colours of the sky bleed like an inkblot, darkening with menace, they inhale their fury. Trunks become twigs, rivers breach their boundaries, cliffs crumble. Storms rage. To give them a name gives them a humanity, that belittles their power, they are not human, they are born out of the primal torrents of the Earth. They rend the curtain of the heavens from top to toe.

The ordinands at the Sri Lankan Methodist Conference give their testimony. These accounts have common threads, the war that split the country by language and ethnicity, and the Tsunami. One man speaks of the night of the storm. His family watched in awe as the sea pulled back and disappeared. Many ran out to get closer to this unknown phenomenon, hungry to claim the land that was emerging before their eyes. And then, that terrible spectacle of a massive wave coming into land, sucking up children, women, fishermen, boats, creatures. Like a massive whale pulling everything into its belly. The fortunate ones spewed into trees, most were simply swallowed into the dark chaos of the Deep. One man describes his unenviable choice, to save either his wife or his mother. This horror has no human name.

I remember my own upbringing in Tenterden, once part of the Cinque Ports Confederation stretching the south coast of Kent and Sussex but subsequently ten miles from the sea due to the dramatic change of course of the River Rother during a great (and unnamed) storm.

I think of my early memories around Romney Marsh, an area still vulnerable to rising water levels. I think of the habitual floods of the Severn and in Hebden Bridge, in Yorkshire. I reflect that we all remain vulnerable to storms, all are held at their mercy even in the most sheltered parts of this cluster of the tiny islands that form Great Britain. I think of those remote parts of these islands, cut off by weather fronts and high tides, with residents grounded or without supplies.

And all those ships cowering on the seabed, graves to fishermen and adventurers, holed by rocks or shell fire , driven to their destruction by the unpredictable violence of many storms. The power of these mighty natural events to change the course not just of rivers but of history itself.

When I face my smallness, powerlessness,
vulnerability and fear
in the face of the storm,
help me to realise again
my insignificance in Creation
and my total dependence on the Creator.

Night Three

We go to bed with a glass of water, drawn from the bathroom tap. This small and mighty gift! We know it is safe and clean, we know that we can stretch out a sleep hand and quaff the dreams to a different place. Such a small thing, such a huge privilege.

Thank you God,
for the rain that has filled the reservoir,
for the pipe leading under the street
to my house,
the stopcocks under the sink,
for the steel cold tap,
for this clear glass
and clean water

Forgive me for taking it for granted,
as I stretch out my hand in the night
to drink it
may I reach out my hand in the day
to those for whom clean water
is not within reach.

4

THE FOURTH DAY - SATURDAY

We have turned it into children's jigsaw puzzles, greetings cards, cartoons, old Father Noah and the two by two of giraffes and elephants. With the rainbow and the dove and the jolly adventure of it all. We have made the rainbow concurrent with the flood, the peaceful dove hovers above the Deep. We have drawn the sting of the utter devastation of the catastrophe, we have told ourselves a benign story as if the world is not broken and flooding and all the animals not in peril. We have turned to look at rainbows as the sea-levels rise to the mountain tops.

We know, of course, that the story of Noah is a myth. That is, it is a story that is not factual but contains truth. We know too that it is a myth with roots outside the narrative of the Jewish Bible alone, it is a thread running through many traditions. We do not know the extent or nature of that historic flood. But the truth it contains cries out to our current understanding of glacial melt and rising sea levels.

We are right to ask ourselves whether God's promise that it will never happen again still holds or whether our covenant relationship with the Creator has been irredeemably broken. Can there ever be a rainbow that says these days of flooding are past for good?

The story tells us that covenant relationships are two-way. God promises because Noah acts. And Noah acts on behalf of the whole of creation, not just for himself and his family, he gathers all living things into the ark, he is the archetype of someone caring for the earth, someone who sees the interdependence of all living things. Someone who both trusts and acts because of his relationship with the Creator.

But we also see God, relinquishing the power of chaos, pointing the bow and arrow of the rainbow at himself as a reminder of his promise. Pointing the bow up towards the heavens.

I don't know whether there was actually a flood in ancient times, although much geological evidence points to the likelihood. But we do know that sea-levels rise year by year and coasts and islands are being washed away.

This causes people to be on the move, not setting sail in an ark but in flimsy boats on precarious journeys. Because where there is flood then there is exodus.

And also, water comes in different floods, in droplets that are sneezed or coughed. Juices that are shared in intimate settings, the exchange of body fluids. The modern flood maybe does take over the whole earth, but puts us all at sea because of the invisible viruses that float and drift on the translucent shores of our intimacy.

We ask again, 'Will God destroy all of us and all of creation, and where are the mountain tops of promise where we hope to see the spectrum of covenant?

Creator of covenant

whose promise to us
still holds,
we turn to you in our vulnerability
as the waters of fear
trouble our societies and our politics.

Remember us, we pray
re-create, renew us, restore us
give us courage to prevail
against floods of doubt and uncertainty.

Bring us to a new relationship with the Earth
and with each other
mindful of our interdependence
and our God-given responsibility.

Night Four

Three o'clock in the morning is such a liminal space, between the exhaustion of the night and the first watery light of dawn. It is a pivot of an hour, where resentment nestles beside longing, anticipation caresses despair.

We are all at sea, dear God
and all around causes anxiety,
fear and threat.
We are just a little boat
on a wide ocean of doubt
in a sea of sorrow,
in the storms of uncertainty.
How come, you can sleep when
the Deep opens up to swallow us,

when all around is threat
and broken promises?
Still me, as you stilled the storm,
wake up and sooth me into a deep sleep
in this betwixt and between place.
Help me,
for there is no other than you
who can or would or needs
to stay in this boat with me.

5

THE FIFTH DAY - SUNDAY

There are moments which put a full stop into time. From then on there will be a 'before' and an 'after'. A war, an assassination, a disaster, a disease, a family tragedy. They are not just events, they are fissures, eruptions, fragmentations and re-configurations of our primal story.

There is always a time we can remember and a time we inhabit but the two are disconnected by this event. What has occurred re-tells and re-frames the events of the past.

Like when the Israelites decided they had had enough exploitation and overnight left their homes and set off on some wild dream of promise. When the sea split open and exploded history, so that their story to freedom could tread dry foot into another sphere. Exodus, the defining moment of a nation and the paradigm shift for the world that follows. The cracking of understanding so that suddenly we, like those migrants into the desert, are suddenly in an entirely new place, unknown, uncharted and unexplored. The coming out of people.

Like all coming out there is a process. I am not who I think I am, I am not what people say that I am, I might be something different, I AM something different, this is who I am! For the ancient Israelites there came the realisation that their identity was not beholden to their overseers in Egypt. On the contrary they were a distinct and chosen people, called to re-find and claim their identity beyond being slaves to systems that sucked them dry. Their journey into discovery, of this new land of promise, led to a wilderness of self-doubt and angst. They had hoped for so much in the leaving of things, but now they needed to enter a barren landscape. It was no longer possible to define themselves by what they were not - we are not slaves to the Egyptians - now they needed to enter the wide open and harsh landscape of discovering who they actually were.

Many, many years later, Jesus enters a similar landscape. The tempter taunts him with the tiny word of self doubt '*if*', an insidious snake of a word. *If* you are who you say you are then surely, Jesus, you don't need to be restricted in your vision of who you are and who you serve. Look! All this could be yours if you wanted!

And we hear "Jesus is thirsty". just as those ancient forebears who are scared that there will not be enough food and drink to sustain them in their wilderness of not knowing, of liminality, of transition, of exodus.

Like the caterpillar that must melt down into its very DNA in order to transition into a butterfly, so these pilgrim people must be reduced to nothing, to fear and trembling, to the ultimate self doubt before they can claim their new being, the coming out people of God , thirsty and confused, on the other side of the sea.

You made the earth out of chaos
and brought us out of the Deep
and so, Creator God
help me to discover
who I really am.
From the chaos of my disordered life
from the depths of my insecurities
lead me through this wilderness
Into the on-going creativity
of this day,

Night Five

God of wisdom, who entered the desert because life was not possible elsewhere, and in that place found solitude, conviction and purpose. I am aware tonight that so much of what I portray to others is not really who I am. Help me to learn from the many people who have come out in various and diverse ways, not to be frightened of the desert landscape which, if I can enter it completely, will reveal my real being.

I am not who people think I am
I am not sure who I am
I might be something else
I am something else!
This is who I am
Thank you , God.

6

THE SIXTH DAY - MONDAY

These are turbulent times. The storms rage, the shores are battered, our defences are down. And yet the psalmist talks of leading us beside still water. Still water? I am wracking my brain to think when or if I have ever been beside water that is still, completely mirror calm. And as I try to recollect what still waters are like, I also sense a sort of dread. 'Still waters run deep'. What is on the surface might deceive, there might be a great abyss down there, a hidden depth that can consume and drown. Do I really want to be beside still waters?

Even though you take me through the valley of the shadow of death, you give me a vision of still waters, where presumably there is the possibility and peace and reflection despite their unknown depths.

As I think, then I do call to mind a stretch of silent unruffled water, even though I cannot recollect when or where it was. Maybe a Scottish loch? Maybe a reservoir somewhere? And what it brings to mind is a profound and all consuming silence, an intake of breath that did not bring a gale of words in its wake. Maybe the depth of still water is not terror but silence?

There are levels of silence, The first sitting with feet on the ground and hands in the lap. The irritation of intruding extraneous noises and thoughts, The interruptions from the mantras of anxiety, did I, didn't I, would I, should I? The attempt to let it go, to let it be, Then silence falls off a step, it goes down a level, it enters a space where words are no longer needed, even within those intruding thoughts. You lead us beside still waters, those of us who sit in this silence together, stepping gently over the edge into the embrace of silence.

I remember where it was now, it was a little lake and we had taken a rowing boat. I had the oars and was happy with the pull and drip of their weight and thrust. We set off with determination but then realised we didn't really have a destination except to leave the shore and be free. So somewhere in the middle of the lake we stopped our banter and teasing and I pulled the oars into the boat. Yes, it was still then. Not silent because birds cawed and circled, squabbled and swooped and the occasional fish flopped on the surface with rings and bubbles. But the waters were still and deep and took us to a different depth of silence.

How to get there, in all this flutter and turmoil of anxieties, real and imagined? How to be led to the still waters, where even the still small voice of the spirit is hushed for a moment. A place where I am not led or guided or directed or instructed or commanded, a place simply to be on this looking glass of water and let that be sufficient.

Let me be silent enough today
to find a moment to be still
and in that stillness

descend into the silent waters
of your grace,
be submerged in your peace
and step down again
into the eternal waters of your love

Night Six

There was an article in the paper today about how to combat insomnia. It talked of breathing deeply from the diaphragm. It made me think of the sea on a summer's evening, the waves coming gently onto the shore and being sucked down through the shingle. It is a noise I love, a reliable rhythm of ebb and flow that speak of the continuity of the ocean over above all the unrest of the land.

I pray this night
for a stillness the other side of tears
for a calm the other side of storms
for gentle waves of peace and sleep
to fall softly on the shore of my anxiety
and enfold me with silence and rest.

7

THE SEVENTH DAY - TUESDAY

The thing about walking a canal tow path is that you don't have to navigate. The path follows the canal and the canal follows the contour lines and after a few days you are friends with the ever present water and it becomes your sure companion.

The canals give every appearance of being straight but in fact it meanders this way and that keeping level with the land. When it needs to rise or fall it calls into action a lock gate, that perfect design of pressure and balance that allows the levels to be equalised. The lock appears solid and still, but with the merest wind of the key and lifting of paddles the torrent of water begins to burst into the dark slimy chamber, and the enclosed boat bobs and lifts until the new equilibrium is reached.

The canal hides the sheer sweat and labour of the navvies and engineers that imagined and formed it. Their bodies measuring, poddling and shovelling the mud, their families a long way away waiting for news and money for food. Many of them dying as they went, An occasional canal-side graveyard marking their passing with scant memorial.

The water is brown and at times shallow with reeds and debris. It has the sullen and polluted air of the towns with whom its downturn in fate is shared. The bridges, scarred by the tug of ropes, echo the plod of the horses that yanked and hauled their industrial cargo to mills and factories. Their arches reflected in shimmering glints as the wind ruffles the surface beneath, framing fields and green meadows with an arch of expectancy. The canal has a memory and reminds us at wharfs and quays that it was the source of resources in a byegone day, when the smoke and silt of the industrial city needed the flow of this artery to bring life and energy, It was a reliable conduit of life.

The canal was a daring act of imagination, born of the confidence of wealth and patriarchy. It was a subversive idea to slice a channel for the movement of industry between the cities and to let goods travel behind the scenes to the augers and shovels of the labour that would unload them. The canal was the bearer of resources, hunks of coal, mineral or clay. It was an audacious bare-faced assumption of power,

Now, it is clogged and claimed by moorhens and coots sitting on rickety nests perched on old tyres or tangles of weeds. There are Celandine bright and brazen, cowslips, tufts of reeds and transient reflections of skittering clouds. There are working parties dredging or collecting litter and neatly painted narrow boats moored outside pubs with tv ariels and pots of geraniums by the logs stacked for the interior stoves,

And yet it is the water that shows the path, takes the route, directs the pace of those who holiday or dwell on its murky surface. The canal shows the way, it is definitely the leader.

On this day, I pray,
for trust in the path ahead of me,
for patience to follow,
for the companionship of the water,
for surprises
and glimpses of new life.

Night Seven

Nights offer us a pause, a break from the conscious and a time to put some commas into our lives. In the canticle of St Francis we hear him speak of 'Sister moon and stars', welcome companions and travellers.

May this dark night be a blessing,
as I thank my sister moon,
and her family of stars,
for their company.
May I see in their dependable presence,
a glimpse of constancy,
of infinite love,
and eternal covenant.

8

THE EIGHTH DAY - WEDNESDAY

Today I was asked to write a reflection. I was reminded of Narcissus, whose great beauty caused him to fall in love with his own reflection and become self-absorbed. Being someone of no great beauty I pondered my own aversion to mirrors. I have no inclination to fall in love with my own reflection, in fact, in my opinion, my reflection does not particularly reflect who I am. Clearly I am at least twenty years younger than my reflection would imply!

An artist knows that in painting a reflection on water it needs to go an equal distance downward to the actual object being reflected. Reflections are deep. They do not skim the surface of water they are held into the depths of the water, they go down and down. And, apart from in jigsaws, they are not an accurate inverse of the object, they are distorted by ripples and colour and the movement of the wind. Reflections are like an object but they are not the object, they are ephemeral, fluid. Reflections are altered by the way in which the surface distorts and shifts, the wind moves the meniscus, the reeds sway, the light glints and glistens on the undulations of the moving water.

The reflection that I was asked to write was concerning my year as President of the Methodist Conference. A year that has had many highlights, deep moments and fun. But also a year disrupted by Brexit, a General Election and Coronavirus. When I look deeply through the many ripples, glints and turbulence of the year, my written reflection is simply a snapshot of a moment beside the river, not an analysis of the intricacies and nuance of all that has come my way at this time.

In doing so, I have also reflected on where I am in all of this, how much the image of myself has been changed by the breeze of the spirit and the turbulence of the age. Unlike Narcissus, when I look into the water at my own face, I do not fall in love, but rather marvel at the transformation of time and experience on the surface and the undercurrents of my life. Maybe I will not call them wrinkles any more but ripples?

This afternoon I have been painting a picture of the sea. I love painting the sky, with all its hues and eddies, with the swirls and movement of wind and rain. Coming to paint the water I know that this must reflect everything above but also has the refraction of light on the surface and the hint of fathomless depth.. Painting sea and sky is an endless conversation in blue and gold, between heaven and hell, between all that we can see and all we can imagine. I look into it and fall in love with this infinite possibility as I struggle with the inadequacies of the paintbrush and my lack of aptitude in representing both what is present and what is total mystery.

In glint and shimmer,

in corners and shadows,
in sunbeams of touch
and intensity of presence,
dance as light on my life,
capricious Spirit.
Cast your insight
into the dark recesses of my soul,
fisherman Son.
Hold me on as the apple of your eye,
artist Father.
Let me walk on the surface tension
of your upholding grace

Night Eight

Days and seasons ebb and flow like tides, reliably, steadily, sometimes stormily, occasional with high points reached or with the undertow of regret. The waters on the beach are like a heart beat, pumping the fluids of creation, bringing life and stability, determined, resolute, primal.

As the light ebbs
and the undertow of the evening
draws us towards sleep,
we ask for the assurance
of the heartbeat of your presence
steadying our pulse,
pulling us back to rest
within the ocean of your love.

9

THE NINTH DAY - THURSDAY

We had been driving out of the city and towards the border for at least four hours. The road no longer had tarmac nor the hectic activity of rickshaws and motorbikes. The hooting of the brightly painted lorries was now intermittent as we bumped and bounced through a day of ever increasing heat. Even the Bishop was no longer talking on his mobile phone but concentrating on the road ahead, there were intense conversations in Urdu with the other passengers which seemed to involve directions and differences of opinions. A few camels were working in the dusty fields and there were small dwellings made of straw and dung.

I realised a long time ago that on trips such as this it was totally necessary to relinquish all control. It was never a 'British day out' where you packed a picnic and went to a chosen destination. If you are in Pakistan then you are always going to take in more things as you go along. You learn always to have more drinking water than you think you will need, the sunscreen, hand gel and probably a cereal bar tucked into your rucksack. This day was no exception.

We were heading for the villages on the India Pakistan border, some of the most remote and poorest communities on earth. We would eventually be greeted by crowds of barefoot children with towsled hair and wide smiles, mesmerised by our peculiar white faces and large hats. This was a rare trip for the other occupants of the car, as well as myself. We had already crammed in an extra passenger in the form of the Christian pastor who worked out here in the soaring heat.

Predictably the conversation involving directions resulted in much arm waving and pointing until we stopped with a judder at the side of the road. 'Barbara' the Bishop announced, 'we will stop here to baptise a baby!'

The church was already crammed when we entered and were garlanded with necklaces of flowers, women in colourful shalwa kameez to one side and a few elderly men to the other - all younger men were out in the fields as the crops could not wait for church services. There was a glass of water on a small table but no sign of a baby.

The Bishop called for the baby to be presented and two women came forward, one elderly and the other drawing from under her flowing dupatta a tiny newborn, "His name is Elias", she said. The grandmother was smiling, she was here to represent the father who could not miss the payment for his day's work for such an event.

I looked around for a font, but the glass of water was the focus. With the smallest of gestures the bishop dipped his hand into the water and Elias was baptised. And then the mother picked up the glass and drank half and passed it to the Grandmother who did likewise. Water should never be wasted in a desert!

For the generosity of small things,
for the journey to surprises,
for the wisdom of those with very little,
I thank you, Creator
and I ask
that I may find you glorious
in the ordinary and small events of my life,
a sparkle in the dusty places,
a drop of dew in the parched places,
a glint of glory in the desert places.

Night Nine

Today we have done a spring clean of the bedroom, knocked down the spiders' webs and hoovered under the bed. We have dusted the lintels and cleaned the windows, neither of us wanted to do it, but now we are glad we did!

Thank you house keeper God for cobwebs
the spiders who design their webs
and thank you for the dust
that settles around us,
reminding us of our mortality.
Thank you for the windows
that when cleared let light shaft in,
views come in,
moonlight come in.
This night, may we rest in this tidy nest
with dreams that settle us
because tomorrow
the spiders will have spun again,
their yarns hang silver again,

the view will fog and cloud again,
muddle will begin again
but you will still be with us.

10

THE TENTH DAY - FRIDAY

Between June 2019 and the same time the following year I was President of the Methodist Conference in Britain, During this time I experienced and learned many things - but in particular I learned a lot about plumbing!

The Methodist President has a 'ministry of visitation' which means that we travel a lot. For me my travels took me to Myanmar, Bangladesh, Zimbabwe, Buenos Aires, and many, many other locations on mainland Britain and the islands that form this archipelago. I experienced and learned many things, gained a multitude of insights and thought about and witnessed the work of God and the Kingdom in many places. One of the side effects of traveling so extensively is that each night is spent in a different venue, either the home of some kind host or a hotel room. And all these locations proffer a variety of plumbing!

If we start with the humble toilet flush, it might be a handle or a button, it might be a string with a handle hanging from a ceiling tank. Then taps, they either pull towards you or away, or move up and down with paddles or possibly you just have to wave at them. We won't mention the toilets without flushes and the contortions involved with a jug of water. Moving swiftly on... who invented a shower that you have to be inside before you can turn it on and be blasted with either freezing or scalding water before you reach the temperature control? Meanwhile hotel showers point in such a direction as to have flooded the whole bathroom before you can determine how the settings work. Plugs can be push down, pull up or seemingly operated by witchcraft. And we won't even begin to discuss hand-dryers which you have to wave at or insert your hands so far into that it looks like your skin came loose in the wash.

Then there is the challenge of remembering where you host told you the bathroom was when you arrived tired and bemused the night before and in your sleepy stupour navigating to it without staggering across the landing into their bedroom or a handy linen cupboard.

I often recollect the time I was in the north of India in the weeks before monsoon season was due to begin. The whole country was thirsty for water and the scant supply was housed in a tank on the roof top of the guest house. Washing went like this. Enter toilet area, use toilet, half- fill a bucket water and begin with your face, washing down your body until you get to your feet, then stand in the bucket, leave other smelly bits until last. When the whole of your anatomy has been washed, then exit the bucket and wash your clothes in it, and finally use the water to wash away the contents of the toilet. One bucket does all! The discipline of managing with half a bucket of water in this way is easier in hot climate but still a challenge. Water is like gold, we should value it that way, however it is delivered!

For baths and showers,
for taps and hoses,
for wells and standpipes,
for bowls and buckets,
for flush and fixtures,
for drips and drenches,
for cups and basins,
for pipes and washers,
for the daily gift of water,
God's holy name be praised!

Night Ten

I started the day being thankful for water and taps and toilets that flush. Tonight I am mindful of those who sleep on our streets and for whom a wash in clean water or the use of a decent toilet is a luxury. It is hard to imagine what it feels like to be sleeping rough night after night, the cold of the pavement and the vulnerability to weather and violence.

Jesus, once homeless and destitute,
refugee and outcast,
criminal and crucified,
help us who are privileged with safety
water and health to be
mindful that this a human right for all people,
whoever they are and wherever they live.
Provoke us to be active
in supporting those who sleep rough,
both in practical ways
and in our prayers of intercession.

11

THE ELEVENTH DAY - SATURDAY

I did once climb up a waterfall. It was in Jamaica and the incentive was to walk upwards from the shore through the cascading water in the warm, balmy heat of the day. Of course, behind the torrent of water careering off the edge of the cliff there is a space, a place of immense privacy and tranquility. A secret, inner zone behind the curtain of the falling water.

Waterfalls are abandonment. The rain that has fallen on plains has seeped and soaked into the land, brooks and streams have gathered in it and collected it like an old woman brushing her step, the water has been garnered. And then released onwards towards ever widening rivers, all downhill, all with the destination of the ocean.

With ever increasing momentum the velocity of the downward tilt foams and froths at the edges of the widening stream. Boats head for the edge, rocks relinquish their authority, water is the queen, eroding and moulding the landscape in her wake. There is no resisting this fecund urge toward the sea. The widening river has no barriers to her descent,

Finally in frantic recklessness she somersaults over the abyss, in a foaming white stream of spume. The water crashes and spits into the ocean, the primal call is acknowledged, the return is made in a frenzy of abandon.

Yet, on the inside of this torrent, between water and cliff, there is a space of total tranquility, a slimy slithering rock-face of calm.

Sitting on a ledge between the water and the cliff, I am overwhelmed with the liminality of this place. It is not quiet, there is the persistent rush of water crashing and tumbling on the outside. On the inside there is the solid face of the rock, covered with the wet algae and tenacious plants that lie hidden in its crevices. There are the cracks and the fissures eroded into the stone, the persistent rub of water and splash. Even the hardest of surfaces bears the mark.

To sit here is to know the in-between place of being a human. Between the wild reckless abandon of nature's gravity and the solid, steadfast yet damaged face of the rock.

When I think about it now, I reflect that so much of life is like this. We are always in transition, neither this nor that, neither here nor there. We have babies and we want them to sit, toddlers and we want them to get to school, school children that we hope will graduate, and so it goes on.

So much of life is an undigested meal, a precipitous journey downstream towards the ocean. Yet even when we are in this torrent of mixed thoughts and emotions, there is also a shelf of stillness if we can pause long enough to find it. Somewhere to sit behind the waterfall. I wonder where that is for me today, that liminal place, the 'not yet' place of calm.

I imagine you are here, God,
behind the waterfall of this day,

beside me on this ledge,
between the torrent
and the rock.
I imagine that you have climbed beside me
to this secret place,
and although it is dank and precipitous
you are holding on.
I imagine,
God of the Deep,
that you are not frightened
either of falling
or drowning,
but that you can sit with me a short while.
And as I sit here,
I imagine that you rend
the curtain of the waterfall,
show me how life is provisional,
reckless, and yet sublimely possible.

Night Eleven

Professor John Hull was an educator, activist, writer and man of faith. He was also blind. He wrote of his journey into blindness and the grief and discovery of transformation it revealed to him. In one very moving passage he describes how he began to 'see' the world again through the rain in a new way as he listened to it falling onto the roof of his conservatory.

In the darkness of this night,
I pray to see the world
in the sounds around,

the music of the rain
as it falls flat-faced on the window,
the shake of the trees' heads
rearranging their hair,
the nestle of the birds on the chimney,
the sigh of the earth resting with me.

12

THE TWELFTH DAY - SUNDAY

In the months before she died, my dearest friend gave me a string of pale blue pearls. Somehow pearls sum up who she was, a beautiful person formed from grit.

Her upbringing was harsh, part of a big family of a Yorkshire coal miner - the one with the shoes got to go to school. She would talk of going with a bucket to the spoil heap to collect waste bits of coal for the family fire. She would talk of her mother managing to feed so many mouths on so little money. And the community that strove and held together through thick and thin, through the closure of the pit, the miners' strike and never having enough to eat.

Eventually, she became the head teacher of a local primary school, she inspired children to flourish to their full potential, many of them coming from challenging homes just as she had done. She worshipped in the local Methodist chapel, she supported the Girl's brigade she fought for the community, she fought through the results of a terrible depression. Her own physical disability caused immense pain.

She was strong and stubborn, determined and exasperating at times. She buried all her brothers and some of her sisters before her lung disease closed her lungs altogether. But not before she had earned an MA and an MBE and been to Buckingham Palace on more than one occasion. She was fierce in her criticism of policies that further disenfranchised the poorest in her community. she fought hard for her town.

We didn't see each other that often as we had divergent and busy lives. And yet we knew at any moment if we lifted the phone or sent a text we could simply pick up where we left off.

When she was recovering from an accident, after which it was debatable whether she would ever walk again, she had started to swim. She went to the local pool and swam and swam, dragging her limp legs behind her. Her upper body was strong after her tough childhood, but her will and determination were stronger. She swam until she could walk.

She believed in God, like a fish believes in water. She knew that whatever came her way she was immersed in God's grace. And that nothing would defeat her, because she was fearless in God's company. Naturally, that confidence and assurance can be scary for others. She could be forthright and indomitable, but underneath all that was a little girl that had to rummage through clinkers to survive.

Through all this she showed me
how God makes pearls.
I thank you today,
for those people
who are neither polished or perfect
but whose deep love
has made them beautiful.

As I bring you
the grit of my life
I ask that it will
be formed into something beautiful
by wave after wave
of your grace.

Night Twelve

Thinking of my dear friend has made me think of all that we love and have to let go .... friends, dreams, aspirations, children and as we let ourselves go into the night, may this relinquishing of things bring rest rather than regret.

For the constancy of friends
thank you, Jesus.
For their remembering of me,
thank you, Father.
For their steadfast and unconditional love,
thank you, Spirit.
Bless each friend of mine tonight.
As I sleep, may they sleep.
Embrace them safely in the open arms
of your peace and grace.
All the lostness of this world,
the grief and sorrow,
I pray that you will hold this night,
take it gently from me,
and hold it in the steadfast trust
of your eternal compassion.

13

THE THIRTEENTH DAY - MONDAY

I am fascinated by small islands, how they sit so low to the water, as if land and ocean are not separated. No more so than on a recent visit to the Isles of Scilly, where the West coast of Britain cracks and crumbles into the sea and yet these little islands maintain their distinct way of life and identities. Like Holy Island, which isn't strictly speaking always an island, these small communities have inflows of tourists along with the tides. For St Mary's this influx of visitors is brought in the summer months by the Scillonian, a ferry for goods as well as people. And island folk know that their livelihood as well as their food supply is dependent on this flat bottomed craft. In rough weather, the Scillonian will not sail and supplies become scarce, that is part of how it is for island people.

Thinking about the ebb and flow of the tides and tourists gives a sense of an island being alive. People talk about 'island life' but there is a very strong connection between the way of living on an island and that natural rhythms around. Supplies come with the incoming tide, people leave with its swell. Storms and high winds cause the island herself to hunker down, doors and windows are closed, it's as though the island herself closes its eyes and puts its hands over its head.

An island community also has its own time, it doesn't rush, it must wait. That is not to say there is not frustration and anger but it is held differently. Island people know each other's business, so it is wise to be circumspect around what is shared. Even illness can't be rushed, because hospitals are on the mainland, consultant's appointments need planning.

I don't want to idealise life on a small island, I think it can be immensely challenging at times and it's not everybody's 'bag'. Communities are literally insular and not everyone can belong. But on the Isles of Scilly, once the tourists have either gone home or shut the doors on their holiday homes, or it is winter time and stormy and the night sky holds its umbrella over this liminal place, then I think heaven is not too far away.

The land surfaces above a blanket of mist
the water blinks, the small boats nod,
the coves take a new breath and yawn,
the inlets stretch their arms to the beach,
the sky rubs her fingers across cloudy eyes.
suggests to the sun it is now time to rise.

So rise!
Let's rise like an island welcomes the dawn
turning the the coastline to golden from grey,
like a a wave hitting rocks,
like a gull in the skies, we rise!

Night Thirteen

I live a long way away from the sea these days, but when I visit the coast I am always reminded of the constant and steadfast rhythm of the waves breaking on the shore. I particularly love the sound the water makes as it is is sucked downwards and backwards through the shingle.

In thinking of the night prayer I call to mind a stay in hospital when through the night a nurse regularly lifted my wrist to check my pulse when I was half asleep.

Thank you this night,
for the steady reassurance of the ocean.
As the rhythm of waves measure
the heartbeat of the darkness,
so you watch over me.
I rest within the grace-filled pulse
of God's steadfast love.
I ask for the trust of letting go for a moment,
to remember that tides ebb and flow
without my effort,
and to be able to relinquish the day
to the night watches of the sea.

14

THE FOURTEENTH DAY - TUESDAY

From the beginning of the day until nightfall people who live on islands such as ours are always interacting with water, we wash ourselves, we drink tea, we clean our clothes and our floors. Water is just ordinary, everywhere, part of the fabric of life. We expect water to be there, to turn on a tap or a hose or a shower and out it pours. We moan when it rains but we know it will, we take water for granted.

We tend to undervalue what is ordinary, after all what is the point of remarking on the unremarkable? We are much more easily seduced by the extraordinary, the surprising, the celebrity, the spectacular. Ordinary things tend not to be newsworthy so they don't grab our attention. But many celebrities have discovered that living life in the headlines is an exhausting business, they long for anonymity for a return to unspectacular days where they are free to move around unnoticed. We rarely give thanks for ordinary things until they are not there, they are just the background noise of life, When did we last thank God for a cup of tea - or a Tuesday?

Tuesdays don't get much celebrity status, they are just another day in the week. Mondays have a certain character as we share the events of the weekend with work colleagues or collect the school books and gym kit and pack the kids off from under our feet. Wednesday has a pivotal feel to it, we are both looking forward and backwards. But Tuesdays? They're well, just ordinary!

But the more I think about 'ordinary' the more I want to celebrate it. After all, I am an ordained person, ordained to the ordinary, to find God in the regular and routine ebb and flow of the days. Yes, also to remember the highs and lows of the Church's year and to accompany people through major life events. But mostly to be under orders means to live an ordinary life.

And it's the ordinary people in life, the matter of fact, get on with it, don't make a fuss sort of people that are the most crucial to holding life together. The care assistants, road cleaners, emptiers of bins, bus drivers, shop assistants .... people who do routine tasks with diligence and care. Reliable people who we see on a day to day basis just getting on with the job in hand, the Tuesday kind of people.

Loving God,
please bless Tuesday.
It is neither the first nor the last,
neither the beginning nor the end,
neither the best nor the worst
as a day of the week.
And bless all those ordinary people
who are middle aged, middle grade,
middle class, or just fair to middling.

Thank you God for the Tuesday people,
who don't give grief
who don't give earache
who don't want to make a fuss
who just get on with the job.
May they know they are loved
and blessed beyond words
and remind me to let them know
(*and to be thankful for Tuesdays!*)

Night Fourteen

Unspectacular days are a blessing when they allow for a regrouping of thoughts and a catching up with the 'to do' list. It's hard not to resent them though, to feel they are a waste of time, as though nothing has happened.

Thank you that you invited me
into this day
to wander through ordinary things
and have enough.
I pray this night
for those known and unknown to me
who have enabled this day
to be safe and ordered enough
for good things to happen.
Thank you for this Tuesday
and all the Tuesday people.

15

THE FIFTEENTH DAY - WEDNESDAY

I am mindful today of my Muslim colleague who is beginning the discipline of Ramadan. In the UK at this time of year these are long days to relinquish food and drink in daylight hours. Through working in interfaith relations I have learned a lot about Islam, but also come to value the moments where the Abrahamic faiths overlap. In particular, as women, we have visited and re-visited the story of Hagar.

As Abraham's slave girl and as a bearer of his son Ishmael, Hagar did not have an easy time. Sarah's jealousy, so the story goes, caused Abraham to exile her and the baby to the desert where she remained alone and parched. The Muslim faith tells of how Hagar ran between two hills searching for water and on the seventh run an angel appeared and a spring of water burst open under her feet. This journey is commemorated in the Haaj and the holy Zam Zam water, still a source of inspiration for Muslim's today.

The story of Hagar, appears in all the Abrahamic texts

but can be overlooked in the telling of the narrative. Yet Hagar's experience of being abandoned and lonely with her child surely questions the patriarchal dominance of Scriptural interpretation, she is a woman who inspires courage and fortitude.

The irony of the story is that even whilst Hagar and Ishmael are dying of thirst, the water they need is immediately beneath their feet. Which makes me ponder the irony of my own quest for what gives life, as it were continually running between two mountains, an activity that surely only makes us even more thirsty!

I wonder where I need to stop and today and allow a spring of water to appear? How will God refresh and save me where I am right now and how it might be possible to draw from the deep well of grace that will be provided?

In our conversations we often move from discussing Hagar to talking about 'the woman at the well' in St John's gospel. We see in both women the rejection and struggle that society has placed upon them. The Samaritan women of the New Testament, is also on the outside of society, clearly considered unsuitable company for those around Jesus. She also has a troubled history in relation to men. Like many women she has the daily task of drawing water for her household and carrying the heavy vessels home. Both Hagar and the unnamed woman at the well were challenged to gather water for survival. Each, in different ways, reveal something of deep significance about the water that sustains all of life.

I pray that today
I will stop running between mountains,
searching,
but will trust you to provide life giving water

from the wells beneath my feet.

Night Fifteen

This morning I started by thinking about the holy significance of water and how we are drawn to the source of water as a place to be with the creator or creation. This is true of all faiths but particularly the Abrahamic traditions where the well is seen as a particular encounter with our spiritual as well as our physical needs.

As the earth darkens
and takes her rest
I imagine what it would be like
to sit by the well with Jesus,
to be seen and known,
understood and honoured
and as I lower the empty bucket
down into these depths
I ask to be filled,
restored and refreshed
with the water of life.

16

THE SIXTEENTH DAY - THURSDAY

Today we bought a new kettle - it was a bargain! It is stupidly exciting!

One of the things that is giving us a ridiculous amount of pleasure is that the kettle is made of clear glass and when the water boils a blue light comes on so that you can see the burbles of the currents that bubble as they burst out into steam and announce boiling point. We have made three cups of coffee, just to watch the kettle, maybe we should get out more?

Of course, the novelty will wear off, soon we will just be 'popping the kettle on' and going to the fridge for milk and the cupboard for tea bags whilst we wait, such is the short-lived nature of our wonder for ordinary things and daly blessings.

It has always been a spiritual discipline to focus on everyday wonders, to be totally present to the moment, to sense God in the here and now. And also a secular discipline of mindfulness in which the distractions of anxiety and projection can be centred on breathing and presence. To be present in the moment brings us to the heart of things, to the exquisite savouring of everyday life, of all that we might consider ordinary.

The boiling of a kettle is a comma in the narrative of the day, a gathering and resting in a staff room or office. Water brings us together in its simple hospitality or presence. It takes time to boil and we need to wait and converse as we are subject to its process. Across the world, communities will gather around the boiling of water. Such a simple ritual is a sacred act, like gathering around a campfire and telling stories.

I wonder how this could translate to a church kitchen, where the serving of refreshments is so often a power struggle over the electric urn. I wonder how the preparation and serving of the church tea and coffee could be as holy as the delivery of the sermon? I remember one church I was part of where the orange squash for the children was kept in the safe, as though we were so protective of our resources that our ability to offer them freely was ruled by fear rather than kindness and generosity.

I think of all the secret joys and fears that have been shared in the waiting time when a kettle is boiling, and the intimacy and companionship of conversations whilst cradling a mug of warm coffee or tea. I think of the cup of tea that I received after I had given birth to our first child, and the one lovingly served after my mother's funeral, I think of the morning cup brought to me each day of childhood by my father and those have put one into my hand as I surface into consciousness even now. And there is a profound gratitude in me for such simple, daily acts of reconnection. So, today, as I watch the water boil and the await the blue light I thank God for the simple act of community that is boiling the kettle.

In the simplest acts of kindness,
in the ordinary times of grace,
open a window on your presence,
I pray.
When acts mean more than words,
presence more than reason,
waiting more than action,
holding more than healing,
come again everyday God.
Open a space
in our pressured lives
to sit with us,
and listen,
so that we may also
do the same.

Night Sixteen

A childhood memory comes back to me. I used to travel with my Dad who led church services as a Methodist preacher and we would go out into Romney Marsh to tiny chapels on some dark winter's nights.

I remember that there was often a central pot-bellied boiler in the centre of the chapel to provide heating and that at the beginning of the service a large flat bottomed kettle would be placed on it. We would sing and read and hear the Scriptures and my Dad would preach his sermon, but the real focus would be that kettle because it would hiss and then burble and finally steam and when it was boiling the service was over - and we would all share tea!

Thank you God for the hospitality
of honest community,
gathered around bread and wine
and water.
Thank you for the cups of friendship
and the sweet company
of good and simple people.
Help me not to overcomplicate your love
but accept warmth
as a gift wherever it is offered.

17

THE SEVENTEENTH DAY - FRIDAY

I learned to swim when my brother took the plug out of my rubber ring. We were in a deep water tank in the south of France, no adults were in the vicinity and the sides of the tank were covered with green slime. I remember seeing the goldfish as I went down, and realising there was no way my 7 year old legs would reach to the bottom, I struck out for the edge, the rest, as they say, is history.

As a result I really love swimming but I am also fearful of water. I have swum in various oceans as well as municipal pools, I have swum in lochs and rivers, but I have always needed to know my route to the edge or at least that one foot can reach something solid. I am not a strong swimmer, but a steady one, I am more of a galleon than a speedboat!

Swimming is all about believing. you can swim. If you doubt it then you can't but if you approach the water believing you can stay on the surface, then you will. I think of this when I hear the story of Peter walking on the water, like a cartoon character walking off a cliff, he can proceed with confidence until he realises what he is doing and doubts - and then he is sunk! Swimming is an act of trust, if we believe the water will uphold us, then it will, as soon as we doubt and flounder about we begin to drown. We have to believe the water can support us, even though it has the potential to overwhelm us.

I find it easier to pray when I am swimming than when I am on dry land. In the water I am acutely aware of my vulnerability, that life has the potential of being terrifying and overwhelming, that I need to trust something that is beyond me.

Swimming reminds me that I am but a small fish in the mighty ocean of the world. It reminds me to trust my total dependence on something deeper and more expansive than my own ability. It also takes me to a liminal place, being between the air and the deep water, I must concentrate on the strokes and each opportunity to breathe. Once I have a pace then I think of all the people that are on my mind and swim a length for them. In the rhythm of swimming I feel close to the heartbeat of the creator who is both mighty and dependable and can let my anxiety for myself and others be released.

As I immerse myself in this day,
deep and mighty one,
uphold me, and keep me afloat.
Help me to trust you
when I am out of my depth,
unsure of the edge
and feeling vulnerable.
Help me to pace this day
by the heartbeat of your love.

Night Seventeen

Human bodies are buoyant and if we can spread ourselves out to form a large enough surface area and relax enough to let the water uphold us, then we can stay on the surface for ages. If we panic and flounder about then we will surely sink!

As immerse myself in sleep.
I commend my spirit
into the ocean of your love.
Let me relax my body and rest in you.
Help me to trust that you will hold me,
and those I care about,
above the worries of this day.
Keep us safe this night
and let us not be overwhelmed
by anything other than your love.

18

THE EIGHTEENTH DAY - SATURDAY

In order to get there I had to fly out of the country. The distance wasn't far but the route was circuitous. From Yangon up to Dhaka in Bangladesh and from there to Cox's Bazar, a coastal resort, a place to go on holiday. From there in a jeep to the refugee camps where over a million Rohingya people seek sanctuary.

Their journey had been different. A fearful flight of women and children when the men were shot or disappeared and villages destroyed. They had picked up their babies and fled and when they got to the river they waded in, holding the little ones above their heads. Some had drowned, some were poisoned by river snakes, all were traumatised.

The refugee camps grew and grew. They were not welcome, who wants a million strangers suddenly arriving, dishevelled and confused? As the refugee camp grew, the sand dunes on which it is perched dwindled, the land eroded, the water supply and sanitation were stretched to the limit. Everybody wanted it not to be their problem.

Then there were floods and the heavy rains entered the

informal dwellings but nobody was allowed to dig foundations because that might imply these people were going to stay. The politicians argued, the water rose and the mud slipped. The aid agencies came.

Aid came in the form of food rations and medical supplies and sanitation kits. The aid agencies flooded in but time went on and gradually as the infrastructure improved they had other emergencies to attend to. The international communities began to get compassion fatigue.

Then there was a cyclone warning. We watched it on the TV screen, the swirling circle of wind pushing across the Bay of Bengal, its speed and direction heading straight for the camps. The trees began to sway and shake, the loose rubbish blew down the road, the motorbikes went more slowly, the aeroplanes were grounded. Everyone held their breath.

In the morning it had passed. It hit the coast of India and caused havoc there, and we were relieved that this was somebody else's disaster. But one day it won't pass and a million misplaced people will be washed away.

Jesus, who was a refugee in Egypt,
and alone in the wilderness,
who had nowhere to lay your head,
have mercy on all those who fear flood
and famine,
who are displaced and unwanted.

Do not forgive us for our territorial warfare,
our forgetfulness,
our compassion fatigue,
until there is a safe place
for all your children to call home.

Night Eighteen

I am mindful of all those who hunker down tonight in makeshift circumstances, for whom the night is cold or dangerous. As I am thankful for the roof over me and the warmth of my own bed, I remember them with a resolve not just to remember but to campaign for justice.

God of this night,
when the world is not what we wish
and so much is unresolved,
approach us with your incoming tide
of grace and forgiveness,
so that when morning comes
we will have
fresh resolve
to remember, to recover
to repent of all that is de-humanising.
Cause us to be sailors
on a sea of change,
revived, resolute and reforming.

19

THE NINETEENTH DAY - SUNDAY

Maybe it was Boney M that brought to our attention the psalm of lament, *By the rivers of Babylon*, and the question, "How can I sing the Lord's song in a strange land?", but I found it a recurring mantra in my sojourns to the local supermarket in Bradford. How is it possible to live in exile and find the 'Lord's song' when we cannot speak in our mother tongue or expect to be understood in a foreign landscape?

A friend of mine, almost fifty years after marrying an Englishman, expressed her deep loneliness at spending so much of her life speaking a language that was not her first and the everyday loneliness of feeling an exile from all those formative stories and experiences that were foundational to her childhood in another European heritage.

The Psalmist enables us to hear of those exiles who sat crying by the rivers of Babylon, estranged from all those that they love dear and the smells and connections of home and we can resonate through the generations with their lostness and loneliness, and ask what song should, could, might we sing into this alien landscape?

Surely Jesus too, in his isolation and lostness in the wilderness recalled that sense of estrangement echoed along the way in the question '"Who do you say that I am?" The alienation of the stranger without landmarks or signposts, alone and afraid, tempted and tantalised by the disconnection between self and place.

The Bible teaches us to love the stranger, but surely we must begin by seeing the strangeness of ourselves, the mendicants who wander hoping for acknowledgement but always detached from our place of belonging.

People of faith always have to leave home and sit on the shores of strange lands and ask what on earth they are doing there and to whom, in heaven's name, do they belong.

The river maybe is the only presence with a clue to the answer. As we sit asking questions of the torrent that flows beneath us and beyond us, the question goes into the waterfall of unknowing and we become present both to our own lostness and our own connection to the people with whom we belong . . . our collective call to home coming.

I am lost
beside this river of desolation,
we are lost
in a land far from home
and yet we remember
on this river bank of tears
that we have come from somewhere to be here
and some day there will be a somewhere
to find from here.

Night Nineteen

It is always a difficult question to answer, "Where is home?", especially if we have lived in many different places and for many different reasons.

I think that few of us are settled and maybe there is truly no homecoming until we find our rest in God?

In the exile of this night,
God of the sojourner,
the wanderer, the vagrant,
let me sense your presence
calling me home
to a place of connection and in-dwelling.
Let my lost and home-sick heart
be embraced
by the one who constantly watches
the horizon for my return.

20

THE TWENTIETH DAY - MONDAY

I am a pastoral theologian who trained in Agriculture so almost by definition I think of people as sheep, to be gathered in, to be enfolded, to be counted. But then I had ten years among the wonderful, eclectic, varied and diverse people of Liverpool and another ten in Bradford, making bread and sharing stories and being challenged in many eccentric and difficult ways, and I realised that the job of the pastor is not so much to count the sheep into a fold as to make sure when they come home they have fresh water.

The image of the church as a watering hole has helped me in the subsequent years of ministry. It is not so important to increase our pastoral count as to nurture the flock, to ensure that when the sheep come to us for nourishment they are given something that sustains, gives life and refreshes their soul. The pastor is there to nurture the sheep, not to own the livestock. We are not here to possess the flock but to sustain it. Too often, people that come to church for the first time feel trapped by the expectations of staying and participating – only if they are nourished yet free to leave will they come again.

Over the course of travelling to various parts of the world I have sat at many watering places. Under the wide expansive skies of Africa I have heard animals approaching in the night and realised alarmingly for the first time I am not top of the food chain! In Pakistan I have seen the dispute of a village community over the rights of a village pond and felt the combative urgency of grazing rights. And, nearer to home I have watched the evening cattle meander down the hill towards the stone trough in the dale, where the local spring slakes their thirst at the end of a ruminating day.

I wonder how the church could me a place of refreshment and respite rather than a place to be enclosed and safe, a place to come to at the end of the day in order to be refreshed rather than fulfil a rota or a preaching plan? I have noticed that if we are able to welcome people and give them exits they are much more likely to return, if we try to hold them and keep them they are more inclined to flee.

Spirit of freedom,
may we sit lightly to our desire
to hold onto patterns that uphold structures
but rather open a watering place
of refreshment and nourishment.

May your church offer living water
and cups overflowing with generous grace
so that we will equip ourselves and others
to baptise the world
Into lives of acceptance and justice.

Night Twenty

I am aware tonight of worrying for my children, even though they are adult I long for them to be held closely. I know that love has to free them and let them be who they are wherever they are.

Let me let go,
of all I try to hold,
as you let me be free
let me let others free.
Yet soon
let us meet at the watering hole,
to tell our stories
and drink from the well of love
that sustains our freedom.

21

THE TWENTY-FIRST DAY - TUESDAY

It had rained all night but I had to be up early to catch the train to Tiverton where a friend was going to meet me to complete the journey to the south coast. As I left the house shortly after 6, I met the man delivering the milk who said the road down was impassable so take the back route. Even this small lane had water across but it was passable and I got to the station for the first small train of the day. As we chugged slowly up the Amber valley it was apparent that the river had burst its banks, there were caravans bobbing about in the fields and black plastic bales caught in the branches of trees.

Coming home became a saga. There was a replacement bus service from Tiverton, the train to Birmingham stopped at Oxford because of cows on the line. All services to Birmingham were eventually cancelled, we were diverted to Reading and from there to London, Marylebone. The last train from St Pancras was an hour late, we went backwards around Leicester and arrived in Derby too late for the connection. The taxi driver took me back to Matlock to claim my car which was surrounded by a carpark full of puddles. Floods everywhere!

But what was an inconvenience for me was devastating for others. A woman had been washed away in the night when her car stalled in a flood. The river Severn had overflowed, the people of Doncaster were baling out yet again. Homes and businesses were destroyed by rising water, slime and mud.

It made me mindful once again of the relief efforts I had seen in Pakistan, where parcels of food and clothing were being transported to the areas that flooded every year, where the rising waters didn't only mean decimation but also disease. When rivers break their banks or where the monsoon falls onto parched earth, we see the destructive potential of water, ruthlessly carrying away livelihoods and lives.

In the book of Isaiah we read , 'When you pass through the waters I will be with you, and when you pass through the rivers they will not sweep over you ...' (Isaiah 43:2) and I wonder how we are to understand this in the light of rising water levels and global warming. The people of Israel may have been able to walk through a parted sea, but how can we trust God as sea levels rise and how can we bring justice to the countries that are most affected by our affluent carbon footprint?

You did not say that the water
would not rise again,
or the rivers burst their banks.
You did not say that the climate
wouldn't change,
or the journeys would be safe,

but you did say that you would be with us
and we would not be overwhelmed.

Help us, wise God,
both to trust you
and to heed the warning,
to be thankful for redemption
but sacrificial in our care for others,
our communities
and the Earth.

Night Twenty-One

When I think again about my journey to England's south coast, I am acutely mindful of those people that enabled me to pass through the waters, the train drivers, taxi driver and the man delivering the milk.I think of that old cartoon where a person is stranded on the roof of a house asking the Lord to save them - a helicopter comes by, and a boat and a man with a ladder but she refuses help from all of them saying that she is waiting for the Lord will save her and eventually at the pearly gates she protests to the Almighty, 'Why didn't you save me?' and the Lord says, "I sent a ladder, a boat and a helicopter!'

Thank you
for those ordinary people
who have kept me safe today,
who in being conscientious and kind
have enabled me to live fully.
I pray this night
that I will be more mindful

of those who take risks
to keep me safe.
I ask for courage
so that I in turn
can enable others
who are in danger of drowning
not to be overwhelmed.

22

THE TWENTY-SECOND DAY - WEDNESDAY

When is a river not a river? The river Todd passes through Alice Springs and yet most of the time it is not there. The river bed curves and twists across the arid landscape but there is no water to be seen, just an indication that there might be some water deep down as the Ghost Gums standing on the bank push their roots deep below the surface. There is also a walkway high over the absent river because once in a blue moon there will be torrential rain and it will fill to the brim - but not this year, or last year either.

But even though the River Todd rarely has water in it, there is an annual regatta - Henley on Todd. This curious occasion involves a series of games, as if there were water. For instance there is a boat race with a bottomless boat and a crew running around on the river bed at top speed. There are pirate ships with cannons and lots of smoke. There is even surfboarding, involving planks and pulleys. A lot of crazy fun is had by all, well not quite all, mostly the white mob.

It is quite tricky to analyse the psychology of such an

occasion! The name indicates an expat whimsy around regattas on the Thames or the Oxford and Cambridge boat race, a memory of 'back home' where rivers have water and give an excuse for an occasion. It might be that a dry river gives a sense of power over the elements, rather like being able to walk up a new road before the cars come. It might be that in a place like Alice, it is necessary to create community gatherings and celebrations because a lot of life is lived in a big empty space and there's a huge journey to the nearest big city.

There is something primal about playing in water, even if there is no water. We are drawn to it and to the places where water and land meet are sacred. Of course the ancestors in this land knew this before any white settlers showed up. The sacred watering places were part of the vision of the Dreaming, an internal landscape of paths and features handed on as they passed through the land, lived in partnership with the natural resources and honoured the land. There is much wisdom in and around Alice Springs.

Meanwhile, most of the liquid around here is beer, and in this heat, that is also welcome!

I thank you for all that is
mysterious this day.
I pray for wisdom
to listen to the rich and varied
stories of my landscape
and to enjoy the
playful, nonsense
and deep insight
offered and shared.

Night Twenty-Two

Since this morning I have been thinking about the painting I bought in Alice that had been painted by an indigenous Australian man currently in gaol near Alice. The painting is made of dots and indicates dingo and kangaroo footprints as well as pathways and watering holes. It is framed with some eucalyptus wood that I gleaned from a fire basket.

I pray this night
for all those confined
or imprisoned
by clashes of culture,
the legacies of colonialism,
expansionism or capitalism.
Forgive our disregard
of indigenous communities
and help us to learn,
from their landscape,
from their stories,
from their memories,
with respect
humility and honour.

23

THE TWENTY-THIRD DAY - THURSDAY

Nobody had explained the implications of being in Yangon during a water festival. It sounded harmless enough, I imagined a water pistol or two, possibly a wet sponge. I didn't expect specially constructed platforms beside the road and power hoses!

The morning had been moving. I had been to the war cemetery, a neatly tended plot with many graves and memorials for soldiers from all around the world who had died during the Second World War. I had in my pocket one of Grandpop's 'dog tags', a medallion to be attached to army uniform with an identification number, the grim fact being that if there was no other part of your shattered body that was recognisable, then at least there was a chance at identification. Even so, the graveyard had many stones marked 'unknown soldier'.

Grandpop had not really been far outside Cornwall before he arrived in Rangoon. He was a simple, kindly soul and told us that he used to shoot to miss because he didn't want to hurt anybody! He didn't really talk much about his experiences except to mention he had a night completely alone in the jungle and woke with a cobra as a pillow and that he saw somebody's head blown off. It was enough to get the picture. I am sure he had no idea what he was doing there.

So, seeing those well tended graves, reading the names of British, Indians, Australians and many others, of many different cultures and religions, was a salutary reminder both of the stupidity of war and the vulnerability of peace. An afternoon of a more carefree nature was called for, so I made the mistake of wandering out of the hotel on my own to see what was going on.

The thing is about a water festival is it's all about going crazy with water. And if water has been in short supply for a number of months and now for a season there is plenty, well you just need to make the most of it! The only thing in my favour was, that as the only white person around, people hesitated for just a moment before emptying the bucket on my head. After a bit, I entered into the fun, after all once you are soaked to the skin, not much else matters, so in that fatal moment of hesitation I learned to grab the bucket and pour it over the offending attacker, much to the glee of all around! And at least in that hot climate nobody is soaked for long.

For humour and honour, I pray,
for sorrow and play,
for shadows and lightness,
for darkness and gentleness,
for sadness and fun,
in all the contrasts of this day
drench us with sunlight,
loving, suffering, laughing God.

Night Twenty-Three

I have been recalling my mother's return from South Africa some years ago when she had made a long saved for trip to visit Aunty Thelma. She described standing at some destination between Cape Point and Cape Agulhas and seeing the meeting of the Atlantic and the Indian oceans, one warm and the other chilly, one blue and the other a turbulent brown.

In this night
I pray for a rest
that allows for contrast,
for contradiction,
for mixed emotions,
and permission to acknowledge this day
has been incomplete
confusing and perplexing
and even so
is now finished.

24

THE TWENTY-FOURTH DAY - FRIDAY

We were going from Delhi to the very North of India to visit a women's weaving cooperative. We had treated ourselves to one night in the Hilton hotel in the city before boarding the train and staying in hostels. The hotel had a rooftop swimming pool. We were glad of the respite from the sun and the dust and to swim at dusk in the otherwise empty pool and listen to the sounds of the city beneath us. We washed away the fatigue of the journey and the next day took on a different direction, a different pace, a different destination.

The train station was chaotic and yet organised. We were part of the hubbub of parcels, chickens, children and businessmen. A woman had a small baby tucked under her sari, a man was asleep against a pile of cotton bales. We set of punctually and sat in the crowded compartment, a source of intrigue because of our white skins and soon with many new friends wanting to chat in English. The day passed, pulling into and out of stations and people boarded with huge plastic bowls on their heads selling snacks and drinks. If you reached out through the grills of the window at a staton you could buy bananas.

We travelled for eight hours and at the end of the line disembarked and found a taxi willing to take us further up into the hills. As we went other people joined us in the cab, and we squashed together and dropped them off further up in the mountains, school children and women who had been shopping and others who chatted with good humour to the driver.

Eventually, after asking directions from many passers by we reached our destination, a village in the foothills of the Himalayas and a simple guest house with a tank on the roof. Our hosts greeted us and fed us and then gently asked us to be very careful with the water from the tank as it was running out and the monsoon had not yet come. Each day our hosts looked out of the windows at the clouds cumulating over the mountains, maybe today the rains will come?

I often think of that experience of waiting for the rains, the dependence and anxiety of not knowing when or if they would come, the discipline of treating every drop of water as if it is your last.

Although I am not short of water today,
make me mindful
of the many who wait for rain
and those who must collect
heavy pails of water
and for those who are thirsty.
May I be thankful
of every drop you give to me
and respect my dependency
on the rain clouds coming to clean,

to heal
and to refresh me

Night Twenty-Four

I have been thinking of my profligate life and all the things that I have but do not need. The things I aspire to which are not important, the things that tempt me that are of no consequence.

As the night comes,
I take off all the trappings of the day
I remove my clothes and shoes
show me, through this relinquishment
of the outer masks and garments
that I can live a simpler life
and trust you to provide all I need
the daily water of life, sufficiency of love.

25

THE TWENTY-FIFTH DAY - SATURDAY

One of the service chaplains was missing from the conference. Nobody knew precisely where he was, even his wife and family except to say he was on board a submarine somewhere deep in the ocean. He was expected to surface again, sometime in a few months probably, until then he was out of sight if not out of mind.

I cannot for a moment imagine what it must be like to be in a submarine at such closely confined quarters with the same people, without daylight and without space to move around. I expect there are moments of intense claustrophobia and frustration, when those around you are just too close or smelly or noisy or irritating for any kind of comfort. That there is a collective homesickness and anxiety as well as camaraderie and discipline.

The role of the chaplains to the services are integral to the life of all three forces. They must train cadets and train themselves. Their role is to support service personnel and their families through the traumas of warfare and the anxieties of risky operations. They are there as pastors but also as prophets, speaking out if there is injustice or bullying. They are also acutely aware of the mental health challenges associated with the service and the need to be vigilant concerning depression or post-traumatic stress. They must administer the last rites to a person, even if there body is in pieces. They must break bad news and rejoice alongside the people they serve. It is no small task.

I wonder where that chaplain is now? What he missed when he was absent for such a long time, his toddler walking, his daughter's school play, his son going to university, his wife's promotion? I wonder how it feels to emerge from the tiny world of a submarine and have to readjust to space and conversation with others. I wonder how it feels to stretch out in a kingsize bed or run around a playing field? How to be a peacemaker and a trusted colleague for extended times of confinement, to be a person of integrity and good humour as well as someone to confide in and trust.

We pray today for people we cannot see,
for the unknown, patient people
who uphold others,
for those who relinquish their own needs
to support and comfort the troubled,
and for the peacemakers,
who in the face of conflict,
risk their own safety,
to live their faith and embody love.

Night Twenty-Five

I have been aware today of people who woke up this morning needing more courage than they felt they had. Especially people who are living in very close quarters with others and are in need of spiritual and emotional space.

God of this night,
as we contemplate the heavens
that you have made,
the vast expanses of the universe,
the stars in their constellations,
keep us mindful of those without a view
unable to see the sky or moon.

Even though we shut our eyes
give us the vision
to sense the extent of your love for us
and the faith to know we are remembered
even in the silence and the darkness.

26

THE TWENTY-SIXTH DAY - MOTHERING SUNDAY

There are many assumptions about labour and birth and one is that we are all born, healthily and robustly to loving and joyful parents. But this is far from the truth. Almost half of all pregnancies in Britain are not planned, and not all of them have filled the expectant parent or parents with delight. Some pregnancies are longed for but never happen. Some are the result of the intrusive and emotional trauma of IVF. Some people choose not to have children, some are unable, some longed for pregnancies are miscarried or end in still birth.

Being pregnant, carrying a child, giving birth to a baby are life changing events. But so are infertility, chosen or reluctant singleness, miscarriage and infant disability or loss. In all these things we are reminded of our vulnerability and fragility. Some may be born joyfully from the breaking of the waters, others into a vale of tears.

On Mothering Sunday we need to be aware of all these things, and also the place of the men who also make decisions about parenting and often feel powerless or side-lined in the birthing of children. How strange that this particular Sunday comes in the middle of Lent!

And yet, maybe how appropriate? In a season where we re-connect with Jesus at the beginning of his ministry, where his relationship with his earthly parents and heavenly father is being explored, we see both his baptism and his tears, the waters of possibility and anguish breaking all around him.

How interesting too that the analogy of 'being born again' is given to Nicodemus, the idea that we must be born both of water and the spirit. Both these births push us out into new surroundings, wet with joy and tears. Both these births transform our comfortable but small worlds through anguish and loss. Both births give us new air to breath and landscapes to explore.

This is a poignant day, much more than daffodils and sentimental cards. It is a day to thank God for our own birth and to mourn the lost and the lostness of life. It is a day for being human in all its hope and complexity, sorrow and grief.

This Mothering Sunday
we thank God for life,
for possibility and for growth.
We remember with sorrow
all those unborn or lost
by abortion, miscarriage or still birth.
We pray for all who are disappointed
because of infertility or genetic complications.
We are thankful for the many forms of family
that are part of the human family
and for our part in it.

Night Twenty-Six

I have been mindful that today is a difficult day for many people and have been thinking about the emotions felt by Mary and Joseph when Jesus was in the wilderness.

We know that we always carry our children,
born and unborn
through the waters of birth and death
that anguish and love
are the same thing,
joy and loss go hand in hand.
Help us to walk
through these turbulent waters
towards new life in your spirit,
that in love and anguish
joy and loss we will
one day find peace and resurrection.

27

THE TWENTY-SEVENTH DAY - MONDAY

One of the few side effects of a virus that has caused much of the world to go into lockdown, is the possibility to focus on activities closer to home. For me it has entailed returning to oil paints, an activity that I have not engaged with since the misfortunes of childhood messes with linseed oil and turpentine. I have been trying to paint the sea.

Why would you paint the sea with oil, surely oil and water do not mix? But the physicality and energy of oil paints are enticing, the texture rich, the hues nuanced, the application takes both body and mind. Of course, it is not an easy subject because water is after all colourless, so all application of paint is a depiction of reflection and movement. The colour of waves and surf is an illusion, the technique is to suggest depth and suck and splash on a flat surface, a two dimensional depiction of an infinitely deep subject. It is no coincidence that the ocean is referred to as The Deep.

The paintings start with a conversation between sea and sky because they exist in relationship with each other, reflecting each other, mirroring the turbulence of the clouds and the waves. Then there is a lot of scratching downwards from the horizontal lines to signify the depth of reflections, the hint that the sea is not just a surface but a fathom below which lie a myriad mysteries. Then, there is the application of clouds, each shadowing and billowing and this in turn causes a return to the sea to add another reflective layer to the surface of the water.

I think that trying to paint the sea is a life time's work, it is never possible to finish there are always new layers and depths to this mysterious dimension, to this call to speak of the unspeakable, to contain the uncontainable. I have not yet achieved anything like the outcome to which I aspire, and like most artists I will probably always remain discontented with the the final canvas. But the process and the struggle and the questions that it brings to me are worth the effort, despite the paint on my trousers and the light switches!

Creator God,
as an artist you alone
could see that your creation was good.
Help us,
who are beset with our own inadequacies
to be co-creators with you
revelling in colour, texture and design
but let the process be the journey
and the question always elusive and tentative.

Night Twenty-Seven

I am sitting in bed looking at a picture I have painted of a galleon, moored alone in an empty sea. I am discontented by some of the marks and brush strokes but it continues to draw my eye.

Fathomless mystery,
you call me into the deep,
to explore the questions of life and death.
In this night,
I ask for a sense of being part of that mystery,
part of that question,
and part of your great ocean of grace.

28

THE TWENTY-EIGHTH DAY - TUESDAY

It makes me chuckle even now, the dilemma of my host in Bali. I was staying in a small family guest house which was set out in traditional format around a central meeting area. There were a series of pointed roofs and open sided buildings around the quadrangle where the family lived and in the central area was the family temple. Each morning my delightful host would say his prayers and perform his religious rituals, he would replace the oil in the lamps and place flowers and other objects around the courtyard.

My visit coincided with the expansion of this small family enterprise to include a swimming pool. The increase in tourist trade in Bali meant that guests wanted to be able to swim at their accommodation as well as the beach and my savvy host had decided that this would be a good investment. So, there were men with spades and shovels, barrowing the soil out of the ground and a large amount of concrete stacked up by the fence. This meant that the walkway between the guesthouse and the tables at which food was served morning and night was blocked and it was necessary for the guests to take a different route for their meals - through the temple.

I had been at the guest house long enough for my host to feel he could confide in me. The problem was this, if a woman who was menstruating went through the temple, he would have to purify it. But how would he know? How could he ask? I did at the time take it with all seriousness and tried to make some sympathetic but probably not too helpful suggestions. His concern was clearly taking its toll as he was often seen pacing about and scratching his head.

After a number of days I could see his face had an easier demeanour. 'I have solved the problem!' he announced, 'I will let everyone go through the temple and then I will ask the gods for forgiveness by making many more offerings!'

I agreed that this sounded like a good plan but did not indicate in any way that women can still swim in swimming pools when they have periods, sufficient unto the day and all that. Ah, the complexities of blood and water!

Loving God,
we thank you
that you have made us from skin and bone,
blood and water,
that Jesus touched people who were 'unclean'
because love is more important than purity
and acceptance more important than rules.

Night Twenty-Eight

I have been thinking all day of the dilemmas that arise around breaking rules and social mores in order to be more kingdom centred. There is a need for rules and boundaries but also to keep finding ways to be more inclusive this is an on-going task.

Open my mind, I pray,
so that those things that seem important,
are transformed by those things
that are eternal,
and as I let go of this day,
help me also to let go of all
that constrains and confines me.
Expand my compassion,
for Jesus' sake.

29

THE TWENTY-NINTH DAY - WEDNESDAY

I am thinking of all those people that have set sail to find different lands. From the Celtic saints who set off in their tiny boats to skirt he coast of Britain and Ireland to the explorers sailing to discover new lands and territories around the globe. I find it hard to imagine setting of in a ship not knowing if you might sail clean off the edge of the earth. Not to mention those with maps and charts that set sail to trade or invade on ships with sails and oars!

Then we think of those who in recent days have set sail across the Mediterranean or the Channel, not initially to find a land of promise but rather to flee a homeland of hostility and danger, refugees from Syria, Eritrea, Afghanistan, Somalia, Iran and so many more places where political regimes or economic hardship have made life intolerable.

One day I was making myself a coffee downstairs in the Bradford project, Touchstone, where I was the team leader and I found a man sitting in reception. When I asked him where he had come from he said, 'Afghanistan', so as the kettle was boiling I asked him how he came to Britain. 'I walked', he said, as if it was the most natural thing in the world.

Many people make many intrepid journeys, some for love and some from desperation, may cross oceans in precarious vessels and cross the sea for sheer terror. Many die, and theoe that live are always aching for a place of belonging, for home. I think of the Syrian refugees that I met at a community project who had to decide which of their children they could bring with them and which had to be left behind. They were unable to speak a lot of English but they were making a rug which depicted their journey and were sewing on buttons for each person making the journey. There were also buttons in the sea for those who had drowned. They cried as the sewed.

Where the waters divide
and the oceans break
on the shores of our hearts,
may we know that
we are all held
in this day,
in the same light
we are all held in the same light.

Night Twenty-Nine

I remember when we moved as a family a few hundred miles to a new part of England, our little son was very homesick. Picking him up in his pyjamas we went out into the garden and pointed to the crescent moon and I said, "Look, there's a new moon'" He looked at me and with the pure disdain reserved for toddlers and said, ‘No Mummy, it’s the same moon we had at our old house!’

Whoever we are,
wherever we travel,
whomsoever we meet,
whatever we suffer,
we all live under the same moon.
Shine this gentle, watery light of the night
into our sleeping
so that we might feel connected
to those we miss, and those we love
and those we see no longer.

30

THE THIRTIETH DAY - THURSDAY

The game was this. You had to strip to the waste and parade about a bit, if you can rustle up some bravado plus a following of some adoring girls, so much the better. It's a hot day at the end of harvest and the paddy field has become a low puddle of rich mud. The banks around it are slippery and the whole village and some tourists have taken the bus out of town to stand as close as possible. The old women have brought out their most colourful sarongs, red and pink, high floral blouses, jewels, big smiles. There is food and drink and music and the spirit of a festival energises the late morning warmth.

The idea is simple. You need to catch a fish, a whiskered carp like fish, as big as you can and bigger than anyone else's. You are going to go about this by diving head first into the mud and reaching into the slimy mess until you can get it between your wet slippery hands and pull it up triumphantly above your head. Everyone else is going to shout and cheer and laugh at your antics and for this one moment you are going to be the hero, a brown, mud-caked, stinking hero. And then you will walk around for the rest of the afternoon with the fish and people will marvel at its size and your bravery.

Then you and all the others will go to the cliff face at the edge of the paddy and stand under the waterfall as the cool clear water gushes over your brown green body and takes all the weed and leeches and roots out of your hair. And you will glisten like a water snake and stand in the late afternoon sun, triumphant and golden.

The next day the women will be back, knee deep, planting the new rice and the ducks will be making solemn procession along the paths that today have been a place of carnival and blessing. Tomorrow the water will return again and the irrigation system will partner with the hot sun to raise the new crop that will be sufficient for this island, along with the river fish and spices. And the seasons will flow on into another until the little girls and lads who have watched your heroics today are stripping to the waste and the young women of today are the grannies in their bright sarongs and the rice is planted for another season.

For simple joy,
for the exuberant fun,
of mud and waterfalls
of rice and fish,
thank you!

Night Thirty

I have been thinking about the season of Lent and how each season of our year has its emotional and spiritual associations. How that, even in this time of penitence there are feast days and deep resonances of joy and how, as time turns on its heel, to remind us of the past and beckon us into the future.

Within this season of penitence
let there be forgiveness,
in this season of my life
may there be blessing,
as winter turns to spring
may there be both memory and promise.

31

THE THIRTY-FIRST DAY - FRIDAY

The day she came back from her father's funeral she wanted none of the food that I offered despite the long and wearisome train journey. She didn't want anything but to sit and be still and not to talk. The next day she asked for clay and she modelled a millstone and shoved something inside that she had written. We let it dry. Then, we went outside and stood by the pond and we waited for the moment. And then with a full-throated, heart-breaking, shriek she lobbed the millstone into the middle of the pond.

The tranquil ducks were very shocked and took flight in an indignant swirl into the grey sky. And we laughed at the catharsis of this invented liturgy, where all that anguish could be hurled into the deep. Her father had been her abuser.

She had read the passage from St Matthew's gospel at the funeral where Jesus tells the listeners that if anyone causes a little one to stumble then it would be better for them to have a large millstone hung around their neck and be drowned in the depths of the sea (Matthew 18:6) and she had read it at the graveside and she had read it for her siblings. And in doing these things she had taken the power back, she had her own voice, she had the last say.

Water is not always about ablution and absolution it can also be about catharsis, on the other side of the water nobody can reach you, nobody can touch you. Water is power, wild freeing, permission-giving energy.

How we try to tame it! We put a small jugful in a font or sprinkle holy water with a twig, we domesticate it in washing-up bowls and sinks, we seek to control something that is ultimately uncontrollable. From water we come and to water we will return, it is our origin and our destiny and a force of fearsome power to both drown and to restore us.

Crying out in anguish
to the elements,
to earth and fire and water
with the noise of un-worded pain,
the water alone will receive
what cannot be spoken.
Water alone has
the power to channel
through rock.
Water alone is not afraid of fire.

Night Thirty-One

The rain has been bucketing down all day and the clouds have sat low over the dale, the earth is turning to mud and the stream flowing through the overgrown blackthorn and sedge of the low pastures. I think of the mess and muddle of life, the sodden complexities of relationships, the tangle of emotions, the need for safe spaces.

Wise One
who, when we are most alone
harbours us,
sustains us,
holds us
within and despite the pain,
keep us safe at shore
this night
protect us,
anchor us.

32

THE THIRTY-SECOND DAY - SATURDAY

Derbyshire is known for its Well Dressing. The wells in question take many forms, some a spring, others a water trough or spout in a wall. In well dressing season, they are garlanded with flower petals which are laid out on clay boards to depict scenes. School children, villages, churches and guilds all participate in decorating the wells. The scenes can be abstract or a depict a local attraction or Biblical story. Well dressing is a curious mixture of the religious, the cultic and the local.

It is thought that, although this was originally a pagan practice, the Derbyshire well dressings have also been a means of commemorating and celebrating the supply of clean fresh water to the villages by people of many faith persuasions and none. On reflection it is seems a pity that our contemporary water pumping stations don't hold the same magic!

I suppose we have always reverenced water. Early civilisations decorated wells and honoured springs. In the Hebrew Bible we hear of wells being places of encounter with God and marking out the geography of the land in relation to those encounters. A spring issued from the staff of Moses, Hagar discovered water beneath her feet, and Jacob's well is referred to in the gospel story of the encounter of Jesus with the Samaritan woman.

Wells and springs not only provided daily water but became associated with healing and miracles. Many are mentioned in the hagiography of the saints such as St Inan's well in Scotland and many more in Cornwall and Ireland. The well was a place of ritual and superstition with pagan rituals as well as Celtic shrines.

The Muslim Haaj is a reminder that wells are also a cause of pilgrimage in many traditions. Many Christians make their way to Walsingham and the Chalice Well in Glastonbury is visited both by pagans and people of many other spiritualities. And tourists find visiting wells both fascinating and healing too, there is a secular form of pilgrimage that comes from an historical interest alone and yet also calms the soul. What are the church font and stoup , if not indoor wells? These holy waters are a source of connection and healing, of acceptance and grace.

Today I ask for eyes
to recognise the healing wells,
the places of connection,
the people who refresh
and to reverence the
sheer beauty
and life-giving
every day gift
of holy water.

Night Thirty-Two

We live at the top of a very steep hill and the water engineers frequently stop outside our house to test the water pressure. It made me think about all the invisible pipes that bring the water to our house and from there into sinks, toilets and taps.

Thanks be to God
for washers and washing machines,
for plumbers and pipes,
for water engineers
and the whole system
of arteries and capillaries
that bring water to our home,
this holy, blessed, ordinary water.

33

THE THIRTY-THIRD DAY - SUNDAY

I started my ministry in Blundellsands, north of Liverpool on the Mersey estuary. In those days the beach was wide and open, to the left the port of Liverpool with its maritime history, place of embarkation for many transAtlantic journeys, place of arrival for so many goods and commodities for the cotton, sugar and slave trades. To the right the sweep of the coast up to Formby and beyond there to Blackpool and the Lakes. Straight ahead, the jut of the Wirral peninsula and beyond there to Ireland and America. Standing on the beach in Blundellsands evoked many thoughts and memories, as the pilot ships, the ferries and the tankers all navigated journeys around the treacherous sand banks.

It was during this time that the sculptor Anthony Gormley proposed the installation that came to be known as Another Place. In Gormley's vision a series of 100 life size iron statues, modelled on the artist's naked body, were to be positioned along the beach looking out to sea. This caused a certain amount of concern and resistance in the local community, this empty beach was an iconic space for getting out of the city and walking, thinking, enjoying water-sports or looking at the birds. Nevertheless the statues were installed.

Each day the statues nearest the sea were covered by the salt water, appearing to be standing up to their knees or shoulders in the incoming tide. Those further up the beach were much photographed and, with a certain amount of imagination and playfulness, were in turn dressed in hats and other paraphernalia as football supporters or local characters, much to the amusement of visitors to the beach. The ice-cream vans saw an increase in trade and those traditional pastimes associated with the beach adjusted around the figures. By the time it came to dismantle the exhibition and to move it to another venue, it had become a well-loved attraction for many, and had also become the habitat for a rare sort of barnacle, both these considerations have led to it becoming a permanent feature of Blundellsands.

Gormley's installation stands knee deep in water on Autumn evenings as the setting sun takes on spectacular orange and crimson hues, which are reflected back onto the surface of the water. It is as if, the ocean itself understands the poignancy of all those who have set sail from here, holds the memories of colonialism and slavery, immigration and trade. It is as if the water has embraced those iron men and made them human.

As the water reflects both light and cloud
so may my day be coloured
by the depth of your love.
As the tide comes in
bringing goods and strangers

so may I embrace this day.
As the barnacles cling
to their new home
and transform it,
may I be hospitable to strangers
and to the strangeness of myself.

Night Thirty-Three

Anthony Gormley's figures at Another Place are submerged between the ocean each day, some completely vanish whilst others further up the beach are less weathered and can see further towards the horizon.

As the tide of sleep
comes over me this night
and the darkness
covers me like the ocean,
I pray for those overwhelmed by the day
that tomorrow they will see the sky
and for those who have had visions
of hope this day
that they will remember to share them
with those who are being overwhelmed.

34

THE THIRTY-FOURTH DAY - MONDAY

We are approaching Holy Week and the drama of the last days of Jesus. It reminds me of my training as a student minister and the service that was part of the Easter preparation. We were divided into worship teams and encouraged to explore the theme of 'foot washing'. There was some resistance. Some protested that it was too intimate to wash another's feet, there were corns and bunions and ingrowing toe nails that people didn't want to reveal, surely hand washing would suffice? The liturgy was negotiated and I was partnered with an Anglican student. We prepared the bowls and towels, we arranged the chair and enabled those who didn't want to participate a way to opt out. We were serious about the moment and the process. And then my colleague muttered, 'You wash and I'll dry!'

We laughed so much about it afterwards. Like we were doing the washing up, like we were negotiating with our husbands or children about the role we would take in this everyday chore. And then my friend said, "The thing is, I realised when I was actually washing the feet, it was so familiar, it was something I had done a million times before!"

Of course! Our baby's tiny feet had been ours to care for as we dried between each pliable toe and dusted with talcum powder. Of course, our own toe nails and athletes foot and wonky toe nails. Of course our elderly parents gnarled and corned feet. Of course, we had done this a million times before! This holy act, this daily ritual, this sacred task, this ordinary care for each other.

We laughed. And we laughed at the liturgical responses: "You wash, I'll dry", just like "He is risen, he is risen indeed!" Hardwired into our minds and souls, the holy daily caring of everyday sacraments.

Jesus washed the disciples feet. It was the most ordinary of things, tired dusty feet in need of care and refreshment. And yet, it is this liturgy of care that marks the beginning of the most holy of weeks.

The ordinary
is the sacred
and the mundane, holy!
This mystery is the ether we breathe
the daily, eternal, routine place of grace.
Bless this day, I pray
with the sacramental act
of putting on my shoes
and following you.

Night Thirty-Four

There have been a lot of demand on my feet today, the walking and standing and holding the balance. I ask for the ablution of the Spirit that my feet may be honoured and refreshed by resting tonight.

Jesus, you show us
that standing firm and holding fast
cost more than we can bear,
so take our weary feet
and wash them with the tears of your sorrow,
the balm of your compassion,
the gentleness of your peace
so that tomorrow
we can continue to walk the via dolorosa
of grace, justice and truth.

35

THE THIRTY-FIFTH DAY - TUESDAY

Thinking about foot washing yesterday has made me ponder the washing of hands today. It has been such a ritual associated with the Covid19 pandemic that we may all have got slightly obsessed with diligently washing our hands throughout the day more frequently than in the past. We have not only used soap and water but sanitiser too and been aware of our touch in new ways.

Of course, hand washing is a routine part of daily life and for those who do not have adequate supplies of clean water the infection rate from disease is hugely increased. But for many hand washing is not simply about physical health but also a spiritual practice. The devout Muslim will perform such ablutions throughout the day in association with prayer and I wonder how it would have been for all of us in the UK to associate the pandemic's call to wash with reciting prayers rather than 'Happy Birthday' as encouraged by the Prime Minister!

Washing of hands is not only a phrase associated with

the absolution of sins and inner purity but also quite the reverse, to wash our hands of something often means not taking responsibility when we should, wanting to be free of the consequences of a decision or action. And this is most clearly embodied by Pontius Pilate in absolving himself of responsibility over the crucifixion of Jesus. An apt reminder that our responsibility cannot be surrendered to a desire for religious or moral purity. To be people of faith often means that we end up getting our hands dirty so that we can fulfil our vocation to serve the poorest and the most vulnerable and to live in the muddied waters of our everyday lives.

The hand washing rituals of the pandemic signify not only a desire to keep ourselves safe but also to keep others free from the disease. We have been challenged again to take responsibility for the well-being of our neighbours, hand washing has brought us to recognise our mutual dependancy for health and community.

As I wash my hands
during the course of today,
may i pause to pray
for neighbours,
for communities,
for those without
fresh water.

As I thank God for this routine
may I pause to pray,
for strength,
for carrying responsibilities,
for those who need me.

As I see the dirty water disappear
may I be glad for cleanliness
but not precious about holiness
until my hands are used to help others
in the messy business of serving you.

Night Thirty-Five

I suppose many of us are guilty of treating our bodies as a vehicle for the rest of us and overlook its aches and pains in order to get on with the day's important business. It is only when something goes wrong that we resent our body's complaints! Maybe the centred act of washing hands and feet can also be a prayer of thankfulness for our body's service and a time to notice its beauty and wonder?

As I wash and dry my hands and feet,
I remember all that they have carried
and held for me
all day
and I am thankful for them.
As I release this day into your hands
I pray I can let go and rest
so that I have open arms to others
and direct my feet to walk with you tomorrow.

36

THE THIRTY-SIXTH DAY - WEDNESDAY

It was a strange conversation to be having in Jamaica of all places, as we stood under the mango tree in the University compound. We had been swimming in the open air pool to cool off from the humid warmth that characterised midday on the island when we met our companion from Tuvalu. We were at a convocation being held by the World Council of Churches around reconciliation and peace with delegates from across the globe. 'Tuvalu is sinking' he said, 'the sea is swallowing up the sand.'

Tuvalu is a series of nine small islands sitting barely three metres above sea level in the Pacific ocean, midway between Hawaii and Australia. Due to sea levels rising and coastal erosion the islands are quickly disappearing, scientists say that they may well be completely gone in the next 50-100 years.

None of us can deny that the environment is changing. They speak of it in the long droughts in Zimbabwe, the fire torn devastation of Australia and the Antarctic surveys. Ice is melting, sea levels are rising, water is being dispersed differently. Some will starve, some will drown and others, like the residents of Tuvalu will become refugees. Our climate crisis cannot be ignored, we are all going to have to live differently. Water is the new politics.

But maybe water was the old politics too? Water is power and the ability to channel and use water has always given more power to the powerful at the expense of the poorest. We built damns to provide water for cities and industries and in doing so flooded whole communities like our Welsh family's home in Capel Celyn, a rural community to the north west of Bala in Gwynedd, Wales as recently as 1965. Like the building of new houses on flood plains at the expense of farmland and greenbelt. Like the redirection of rivers to service industries or to beautify the landscape for those with money to buy a view. Like the corruption that causes some to prosper whilst others carry buckets from a standpipe. Like children bottle-fed and subject to to water born illness so that powdered milk can be successfully marketed.

Our friend shakes his head, 'How to change things?' he asks nobody in particular, 'whatever will we do?.' We walk on together to the next seminar, earnest informed people fervently wishing we had the answer and knowing we don't.

Sometimes forgiveness is all we can ask for,
yet we want justice,
we want contrition,
we want wisdom.
To repent, to comprehend,
to turn again,
away from the well of tears,
and towards the well of life.

Night Thirty-Six

The day has passed and again I have boiled the glass kettle with the blue light, run the bath, washed the dishes, taken water to be a given for the day. I am sorry that this privilege has not struck me as privilege but as normal and I have not been challenged to question why I should have all these things when others do not.

After this night I pray
wake me up!
Wake me up to the vulnerability
of all those who are suffering
through climate change,
or the power that water gives,
the power that water takes away.

Give me an unquenchable passion for justice.
Cajole me to hear the uncomfortable stories
about climate change,
to do everything in my power,
with the power of others
to find an equitable sharing of water.

37

THE THIRTY-SEVENTH DAY - THURSDAY

When Aunty Thelma married and set off for South Africa shortly after the end of the second world war, she took leave of her siblings and her parents on a ship bound for the Cape. The journey took her six weeks and after she had got there and slept a little and acclimatised to her new married life, she was able to post an air letter home.

Meanwhile back in Britain, my Mum, her sister waited anxiously for news. It came in the form of a slim blue form shaped into an envelope, crammed with news written in biro and often with very small writing that went vertically up the side of the main page to fill every possible space on the trie-folded missive. For my mother this great ocean that separated her from her sister was vast in a way that it is hard to imagine in these days of e-mails and jet travel. Water was a huge physical and emotional gulf between the sisters, communication was infrequent and precious, they could afford a brief phone call at Christmas.

It is easy for us, who can talk daily with relatives around

the world and get most places within a few days, to forget that the oceans that cover the planet are wide and wild. It is is hard to imagine the intrepid nature of sea travel even today, where ships are wrecked or caught in storms, where fishing boats are smashed to pieces or coastal dwellings washed away in a night's storm. Yet we are reminded of the sea's treachery as we hear of the many refugees who lose their lives trying to cross the Channel in small boats, even such a short journey is treacherous.

My mother taught us to respect the sea, to honour it but not to trust it. Walking on Camber sands could be a happy childhood pastime but the currents could come around and cut you off from the land when you weren't looking. They say that the tide in Cleethorpes comes in at the speed of a galloping horse and can quickly surround the unexpected without a route back to the shore. The sea is our companion but not our friend, it can shift moods unmercifully, there is invisible and deadly quicksand, it can drown us.

When I consider the ocean,
the wild turbulence of its surface,
the dark fathoms of its depths,
the attraction of its shallows
and the expanse of its reach,
I sense my aloneness and vulnerability
before this vast mystery.
For those separated by the water, I pray,
for those in danger on the water, I pray,
that we will not be overwhelmed, I pray.

Night Thirty-Seven

I am mindful of all those who work through the night, especially those who are not on dry land, on oil rigs, supertankers, cruise ships or in small boats in the dark. I think of the families in the hands of traffickers hoping for a new life as they make precarious journeys to new countries.

As I pray for calm and rest tonight,
I pray for safe passage
for all who journey on the open seas
or who fear drowning in oceans
of doubt and fear.
I ask for a welcoming heart,
a safe harbour,
for a homecoming
for all who travel through the dark hours
in small boats.

38

THE THIRTY-EIGHTH DAY - FRIDAY

Each year the Swifts arrive back in Derbyshire on just about the same day. When we hear them swooping above us in the early evening with their characteristic chatter we know that Summer has also arrived. We love to sit in the garden into the late evening listening to these extraordinary birds.

Swifts never land, except when on the nest. The spend their entire life on the wing, migrating huge distances each year with their beaks agape to catch small insects as they go. We watch them swoop straight in under our eaves, in the mornings we listen to the arrival of food for the newly hatched young, we try but always fail to count them. Swifts are in their element in the air, they are at home in the sky not on the land.

Just as a Swift is at home in the air and a herring in the wide expanses of the sea, humans make their home on land. We are in our element, on our two feet on streets or on foot-paths, driving vehicles or tilling the soil. We try to master the other elements but we are not really cut out for it, we are awkward in water and know that it is more powerful than we are and our attempts at flight are clumsy and fuel limited.

If this seems like stating the obvious, it is because I am pondering about our perception that we dominate the Earth, that we own it, that somehow we are in control. Yet it is only through recognising that we are dependent on the Earth, that it is a mystery to us and that we cannot dominate it that creation is going to survive.

Swifts drink by catching raindrops in the air or skimming over water and catching moisture from the surface. These graceful and delicate birds show us the dependency we all have on the elements, the balance of the water cycle, the polar ice cap. It is raining today and I am a bit grumpy about it, but I am going to try to be thankful for these clouds, for this water, for this nourishment, for this balancing of the elements.

For dew and frost,
for rivers and streams,
for clouds and waterfalls,
for torrents and downpours,
for the water that soaks and nourishes this day
I thank you —
anyway!

Night Thirty-Eight

There was a small child in a snowsuit and wellingtons in the market. Her mother was pushing the empty pushchair whilst she jumped into puddles. It reminded me of the sheer delight of splashing in water wherever we find it, from a paddling pool to a hot spring, from a muddy puddle to a burbling brook.

Thank you, God, for puddles
the muddy ones,
the frozen ones,
the rockpools,
the paddling pools,
these joyful gifts,
these splashes of fun.

39

THE THIRTY-NINTH DAY - SATURDAY

Artists have always been fascinated by water and light and the interaction between the two. Water glints with light, light rebounds from the water's surface. From the canals of Venice to the Cumbrian lakes, from Monet's lily ponds, Seurat's bathers, to the storms and gullies of Turner's seascapes and mountain scenes, water and light have gone hand in hand.

Jesus too sailed on lakes and noticed the light's play on life, made wine from water and expected others to walk on it, rode the storms and shed his tears and ultimately and finally had water flowing from the pierced side of his suffering, love and grief. Water and light, they are the great covenant of the elements, sharing each other's beauty, sharing each other's exquisite anguish. Light on water, water reflecting light.

I asked a friend what water meant to her and she said, "It means life!" It seems too simple and too obvious and yet this elemental truth is at the heart of our physical and spiritual survival. Without water to drink we quickly go crazy, without water to irrigate we starve, without a relationship with that which is other than ourselves our lives are parched and cannot flourish. Water means life.

And water brings beauty, in its reflected hues and movement. We are drawn to it, to gaze into it, to wonder at its power and terror as well as its serene stillness. We skim stones on it or pull fish out of it, we jump in puddles and blow bubbles, we go wild-water swimming or set off on liners across it, in so many ways water shows us the glorious scope of the creator in the simplest and most beautiful of forms. Our relationship with water is primal Water opens up the vast expanses of life in all its fullness.

As I stand on the shore, looking out over the sea that curls and sucks at my feet, I sense the smallness of my life in relation to the mighty imagination at the heart of creation, I am awestruck at this beautiful, terrifying, force that with tide and torrent is the heartbeat of the Earth.

I am as small as a drop of water
in the ocean of creation,
as small as a tiny shell
on this great shore.

I am made from beauty and terror,
from power and possibility
in all this wonder and pondering.
Thank you creator, spirit, living water.

Night Thirty-Nine

I am aware that the pondering on water have been a time of personal reflection for me as we approach Holy Week and

Easter and I have been glad of the discipline of writing them. I feel there is so much more to be said and discovered!

Jesus, who by your obedient life
turned tears into a fountain of love,
who turned water into wine that all could
feast,
who told frightened people to walk on water,
who stilled the storm and healed the sick,
I pray, that as we enter Holy Week,
you will anoint us again with water and the
spirit
so that we, and all your people
will know the presence
of your compassion and enduring hope.

40

THE FORTIETH DAY - SUNDAY

Our relationship with water is elemental. Water gives us life, each day we are sustained by it, from our early morning tea or coffee to our late night glass of water. It cleanses us and keeps us healthy, it causes the blood to course through our veins our food to be digested. It cleanses our system, it lubricates our mouths, it cleans our cuts. Yet even though we are totally dependent on it , we do not own it. Water belongs to the Earth, to all people, to all creation. It is entrusted to us to use wisely and justly, it is our responsibility not our property.

Sitting by a well, thirsty and without a bucket, Jesus embodies this dependency and this knowledge. In his conversation with the Samaritan women, he shows us that in the sharing of the water a great well of wisdom is opened up, he shows us that water not only gives life it IS life, it is the thirst quenching gift of the Spirit of God within us.

We know that Jesus was often thirsty, that he wept, that he set sail in small boats, that he watched the fishermen from the shore. We can imagine that he looked out over Galilee and pondered the relationship between his heavenly father and the people who hungered and thirsted for direction and faith. We hear that he washed feet and spat on the ground to heal the sick, that he calmed storms on the turbulent seas. But much more than this, he declared himself to be the living water, that his presence could slake our spiritual thirst, that through water and the spirit we could be born again into a new life with him.

The ordinary water that surrounds our lives, this living water that is promised by Jesus, is our hope. It carries fear and inspires awe, it shows us both our significance and our insignificance in the whole of creation, offering rivulets of new understanding and challenges us to live our lives in a covenant relationship with the creator who both loves us and gives us responsibility. Water baptises us into this relationship with each other and with the whole earth, and I for one, am thankful!

Jesus of the water's edge,
baptise my life with your love,
that all ordinary things will be holy things,
all encounters will be filled to the brim with
    grace,
all creation will be watered and nourished,
that rivers of righteousness and justice
will flow like an ever living stream!

Night Forty

We stand on the edge of Holy Week, like those first disciples, hoping for so much and yet fearful of so much. We inhabit a breathtakingly beautiful world, full of intricacy and complexity, finely balanced, awash with possibility. Yet we also know that we must live differently, shed tears of contrition, make do with less if we are to flourish and creation be sustained. My prayer is that this writing will have helped bring to mind the ordinary miracle of water, its transformative potential and its political power and in so doing, we might turn again to honour it and share it because — from water we come and to water we will return.

As the night pulls the blankets of darkness
around this writing,
as these the words, like water come to shore,
as the earth turns and rests
and the ocean covers the edges of the world,
may your living water
transform these prayers
into life giving water.

May righteousness and justice
flow on the Earth again
as streams of healing and hope.

Amen.

ABOUT THE AUTHOR

In June 2020, Barbara Glasson became the President of the Methodist Conference in Britain. This was always going to be an interesting year, with visits around the British Isles and to partner churches in Myanmar, Bangladesh, Zimbabwe, Argentina and the Middle East in the diary but nobody could have anticipated quite how strange it would turn out to be as Covid19 brought plans and travels to a halt. Returning to a love of writing (she has written over 9 books) Barbara in lock down reflected on a life-time's experiences at home and overseas. The pages reflect both her love of her home in Derbyshire and her visits overseas, her early training in agricultural sciences and her upbringing on the Kentish coast, the development of her pastoral insights in Liverpool and Bradford and her whimsical take on the ordinary things of life.

Barbara is currently teaching pastoral theology at the Queens Foundation in Birmingham and learning to paint and weave in her spare time. She lives in Derbyshire with her husband David and a sheepdog called Seth.